ART LAB FOR KIDS

express yourself

52 Creative Adventures
to Find Your Voice Through Drawing,
Painting, Mixed Media & Sculpture

Follow-up
to the best-selling
ART LAB FOR KIDS

All new
projects!

SUSAN SCHWAKE

Quarto
Knows

Inspiring | Educating | Creating | Entertaining

Brimming with creative inspiration, how-to projects, and useful information to enrich your everyday life, Quarto Knows is a favorite destination for those pursuing their interests and passions. Visit our site and dig deeper with our books into your area of interest: Quarto Creates, Quarto Cooks, Quarto Homes, Quarto Lives, Quarto Drives, Quarto Explores, Quarto Gifts, or Quarto Kids.

First Published in 2019 by Quarry Books, an imprint of The Quarto Group,
100 Cummings Center, Suite 265-D, Beverly, MA 01915, USA.
T (978) 282-9590 F (978) 283-2742 QuartoKnows.com

Quarry Books titles are also available at discount for retail, wholesale, promotional, and bulk purchase. For details, contact the Special Sales Manager by email at specialsales@quarto.com or by mail at The Quarto Group, Attn: Special Sales Manager, 401 Second Avenue North, Suite 310, Minneapolis, MN 55401, USA.

10 9 8 7 6 5 4 3 2 1

ISBN: 978-1-63159-592-9

Digital edition published in 2019
eISBN: 978-1-63159-593-6

Library of Congress Cataloging-in-Publication Data

Names: Schwake, Susan, author.
Title: Art lab for kids--express yourself! : 52 creative adventures to find
   your voice through drawing, painting, mixed media, and sculpture / Susan
   Schwake.
Description: Beverly, MA : Quarry Books, 2018.
Identifiers: LCCN 2018032883 | ISBN 9781631595929 (flexi-bind)
Subjects: LCSH: Art--Technique--Juvenile literature. | Drawing--Juvenile
   literature. | Painting--Juvenile literature. | Mixed media (Art)--Juvenile
   literature. | Sculpture--Juvenile literature.
Classification: LCC N7440 .S3925 2019 | DDC 700--dc23 LC record available at https://lccn.loc.gov/2018032883

Design and Page Layout: Megan Jones Design
Photography: Rainer Schwake; photos in the gallery of artists courtesy of the respective artists.

Printed in China

For Rainer, whose unconditional love sees me through.

CONTENTS

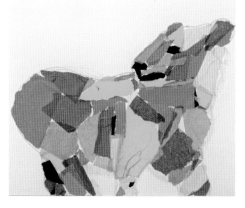

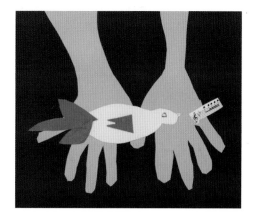

UNIT
1

GETTING STARTED

Beginnings are exciting places to be when you start a creative adventure! This book is a road map for the unique journey that begins and ends with you. The best art adventures are those that come from your own ideas and experiences. Fresh white paper, new boxes of color, and a full bottle of glue can be great inspirations. Sometimes it's puzzling, though, how to bring your own ideas to paint and paper. This book helps you think through your ideas, find your voice, and express your individual style. Each lesson begins with a question, and through an artistic process with a variety of materials, each reader will craft a unique answer. Along the journey, the same question asked another time can yield a completely new, one-of-a-kind result.

WHY SHOULD WE CARE ABOUT SELF-EXPRESSION?

Imagining something and then feeling comfortable enough taking the risk to act on an idea is the essence of *self-expression*. As children, we learn by doing and exploring the "what ifs" of the world. *What if I jump from rock to rock to get to the other side? What if I use these twigs—can I make a nest like a bird? What if I paint all the colors from my paint box on top of each other?*

As a guide or teacher in this artistic process, we must create a nurturing environment with space to explore materials and methods in a process-rich fashion. The single most important objective in the process could be allowing each child the freedom to see an idea through from imagination to creation, without outside interference or judgment along the way. Trying out new materials and methods should feel playful and experimental. End products are less important than the process. Art processes are meant to be practiced over and over, changing things at the maker's discretion. Practicing the process of art making leads to creativity and builds a strong sense of self.

What do we gain from nurturing self-expression? A child practicing making art also practices decision making and working through problems within the process. Creating visual art from an imagined idea can be a powerful boost in self-awareness and self-worth. Self-expression grows from a place of confidence, trust, and truth.

Making art gives you a space to create a visual presentation of your imagination. Art is an important way of communicating feelings and ideas and more: It opens up an inner dialogue. Expressing yourself helps the developing self and nurtures emotional strength. Opening up to art with playfulness and curiosity promotes discovery of who you are and where you want to go. Art opens up new ways to see the world.

We want to value art not by measuring how exactly to reproduce the (outside) world, but to value it for the art itself, for the process, the act of creating, the glimpse of an *inside* view and the sparks of inspiration. What better art is there than art that is touching and connecting with your vision of the world?

HOW TO USE THIS BOOK

This book was written to inspire the teacher, parent, childcare provider, grandparent, and anyone who wants to make art with (and possibly alongside) a child. It is always about the process in our studio—and enjoying the process deeply. For children, art is a way to convey their experiences and feelings about the world. It helps them define and evaluate their world. Sometimes, art making doesn't go as planned and the end product doesn't work out as envisioned—that's okay. It takes a lot of practice! These lessons are designed to repeat over and over to gain competency through repetition, expand creative thought, and increase the maker's skills. I have found as a teacher of both children and adults that everyone learns through practice. I encourage students of all ages to try the same lesson twice, at the very least, and let new-found knowledge guide the process. I encourage you, the adult, to work alongside the students to discover the joy of the process for yourself. Investigate your creativity again and help explain, without words, your world.

The following art materials list is a guide to often-used materials and a simple art studio setup. It is a comprehensive list for all the lessons in the book, but you don't need all the materials for each lesson. Each lesson outlines the materials needed to create the project.

I encourage you to set up an area to exhibit and celebrate the art that is made. This elevates the process to a place to be admired and remembered. A simple string with clothespins to hang flat work can fit in the tiniest of spaces. A shelf or table can hold sculptural work. For larger rooms, a cork strip or wire curtain rod can run along a wall to hold a classroom full of artwork.

It is important to celebrate the creative process without making it all too precious. I often have parents lament about where to display or how to keep artwork in their homes. One of the easiest ways to hold on to the work is to photograph it and have a simple photo book made. We found this to be a great solution for many families. We also gave special pieces to relatives who would appreciate the artwork. Sometimes, I have asked my own children if they have art they would like to recycle into bookmarks or greeting cards. This has been a fun way to enjoy the initial artwork once again by making something new and spreading the love to friends. At the end of each year, in our home, I went through the art that was made and kept one piece for myself and one for each child. These pieces went into paper portfolios and we often pull them out for a look. The rest is photographed and the originals are recycled.

Many of the lessons in this book can be adapted with your own ideas. I think of them as springboards for interpretation. There are many ways that each lesson can be done—be open and let your personal expression flow freely! In a classroom setting, there can be as many outcomes to each lesson as there are students. Most of all, enjoy the process. Embrace the differences and then admire the results! It is my greatest hope that these lessons inspire art making and a closer look at the world within each of us.

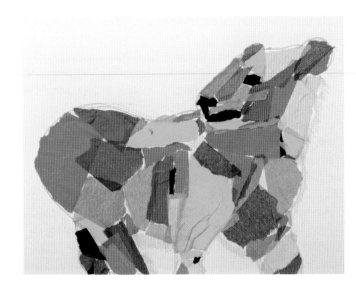

ART MATERIALS LIST

The following list of items will help you build your art-making space. From simple furnishings to basic materials, this list will get you started. Collecting these supplies over time is easiest and most cost effective; however, you may already have many of these items on hand. Don't be daunted by the list—just collect as you can and once people know you are collecting, they will save special items for you! Keep supplies in labeled boxes on shelves for easy storage or in open bins in a corner for easy access. Our studio has a combination of pull-out clear drawers and shelves for items we use often and trays and bins for specialty supplies.

Materials

- ▸ Plastic tablecloths for drop cloths
- ▸ Newspaper is used in many lessons: to protect the table, to dry brushes, to wipe excess paint from brushes, as support for printmaking processes, to dry and clean brayers, as a place to apply glue, as an art material—it's always good to have on hand!
- ▸ Paper plates, Plexiglas, wax paper, or a baking sheet for a paint palette
- ▸ Plastic wrap and aluminum foil
- ▸ Found objects such as bottle caps, buttons, fabric scraps, small boxes, corks, plastics of all sorts, shells, pebbles, tiny toys, ribbon, etc., sorted into labeled bags or jars
- ▸ Screwdriver, nails, hammer, foam brushes
- ▸ Liquid soap, wooden spoons, sponges, straws, rags, clean recycled foam trays from the grocery store, netted bags from produce, clean plastic containers, and plastic cutlery
- ▸ Papers of all sorts—mat board, foam core, old artwork, discarded books and magazines, colored papers, tissue paper, old security envelopes, junk mail, sheet music, catalogs, other interesting recycled papers
- ▸ Adhesives such as white glue, clear glue, glue sticks (UHU is my favorite), contact cement, hot glue, and wood glue are all handy to have. **Note:** When gluing paper, we recommend UHU glue sticks. They work well and last long. White glue is great for lightweight materials such as feathers and yarn. Tacky Glue is what we use to glue on pebbles and button-weight materials. Hot glue is for fast tacking or when we can't wait for something to dry.

- Canvas boards, canvas, plywood, found wood, and fiberboard—all primed for painting with acrylic gesso, or primed with leftover house paint
- Oil pastels, crayons, watercolor paints, acrylic paints, paint markers, graphite pencils, colored pencils, tempera paint, and colorful permanent markers and gel pens for color. Buy the best you can afford. Liquid watercolors are nice, too.
- Brushes of all sorts—foam, bristle, nylon and foam brayers, hard and soft brayers for printmaking
- Scissors, hole punches, and craft knives (*to be used by or with an adult*)
- Oven-bake clay, which comes in many brands, is pliable clay that doesn't dry out and can be hardened by baking it in your kitchen oven according to directions on the package. We use Sculpey with great success.

Having a dedicated studio is a luxury that many students do not have. It is simple, however, to make a small studio most anywhere that can facilitate great art making! Here are a few suggestions for making a comfortable art-making area where creativity can run wild and no one worries about it.

Art-Making Space

Find an area where a surface can be cleared for working. This surface should be equipped with a chair that is the proper height for the student (feet on the floor and waist-high surface top). The area does not have to be large or permanent. A folding table will do!

- There should be plenty of light from windows or lamps or both.
- Cover the surface with either newspaper or a plastic tablecloth.
- If the floor below the table is not easily cleaned, you may cover it with a tarp or plastic tablecloth.
- Have an apron or old T-shirt handy for each artist.
- Store your materials in bins, on trays, or in jars on nearby shelves if you have them. If shelves are not available, a large box or basket can store away materials and yet be handy to pull out when needed. I love using trays! I use them to organize my supplies on my shelves and to bring the specific materials I need for a lesson to the work area.
- You'll need a source for water—a sink is ideal, but a bucket of clean water and a bucket for wastewater work well, too!

EXPRESS YOURSELF WITH DRAWING

"Art is a line around your thoughts."
—GUSTAV KLIMT

Drawing can be as simple as the act of using a stick in the sand or your finger in the air. Everyone I have encountered in teaching art seems to have a unique doodle or mark that comes to the surface in their art. These labs were created with self-exploration in mind; some are processes of practice that yield experience instead of product. All can be repeated over and over with different results each time. Each lab allows the student to make choices—from subject matter to composition and color among others. These decisions make the process a practice of *self-expression*.

Throughout the chapter, we will use many different materials to draw with, to expand your idea of drawing, and find the fun in art making. Trying out new materials can often spark a new way to express yourself. Put perfection aside and let the play begin!

INK STICK DRAWINGS

MATERIALS

▸ wooden toothpick, craft stick, or skewer
▸ india ink
▸ smooth paper

💡 WHAT DO YOU THINK?

What kinds of tools do you think people used in ancient times to draw with? What kinds of pictures do you think they drew? Did you know you can draw with a wooden stick? Let's draw your favorite animal or your pet with a stick and some ink!

Fig. 1

Fig. 2

Fig. 3

Fig. 4

LET'S GO!

1. Dip your stick into the ink to wet the bottom third of the stick. (Fig. 1.)

2. Make a few practice marks on your paper to get used to the stick. Don't press too hard—just let it flow. (Fig. 2.)

3. When you have finished practicing, take a new sheet of paper and begin drawing your animal. (Fig. 3.)

4. Try using dots, thick and thin lines, and short and long lines!

5. Finish the animal and decide what else you want to show in the drawing. Our student drew a second animal. What will you draw? (Fig. 4.)

RIGHT HAND, LEFT HAND

MATERIALS

- ▸ 2 apples or other fruit
- ▸ markers in 2 colors
- ▸ paper

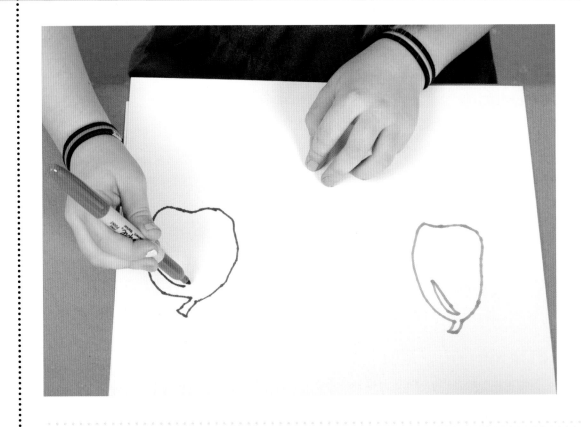

💡 WHAT DO YOU THINK?

Are you right handed, left handed, or both? Have you ever tried to draw with both hands at the same time? In this lesson, you will find out a lot about your right and left hands!

Fig. 1

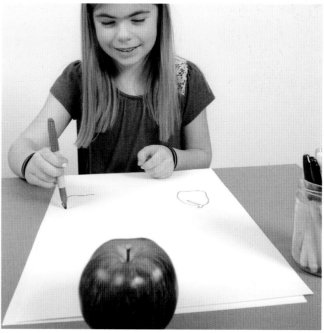
Fig. 2

Fig. 3

LET'S GO!

1. Place the two fruits across from where you are sitting to draw.

2. Choose a different colored marker for each hand.

3. While looking at one of the fruits, draw the contour, or outline, first with one hand and then with the other hand. (Fig. 1.) Repeat this a few times.

4. Now draw the other fruit in the same manner. (Fig. 2.)

5. For an extra challenge, draw one fruit with your left hand and the second fruit with your right hand—at the same time! (Fig. 3.)

BLIND PORTRAITS

MATERIALS

▸ a friend
▸ fine-point black marker
▸ paper

💡 WHAT DO YOU THINK?

Have you ever made a drawing without looking at your hand while drawing? You can learn a lot just from trusting your eye to tell your hand what to do! Ask a friend to be your model and then switch places and be theirs!

Fig. 1

Fig. 2

Fig. 3

Fig. 4

LET'S GO!

1. Begin by having your model sit across from you.

2. Place your marker at the top section of your paper, as you will start your drawing with the top of their head. (Fig. 1.)

3. Keeping your eyes on your friend, begin drawing what you see. *Do not look at your hand*! It takes awhile to get used to this process, so don't give up.

4. Continue the drawing by keeping your eyes on your friend. Notice the shapes and lines you see in their face and hair. (Fig. 2.)

5. When you are done with the drawing, take a look! The results are surprising and sometimes silly. This is a really great way to train your hand to draw what you see. (Fig. 3.)

6. It's fun to try two or three drawings and then give your friend a turn to draw! (Fig. 4.)

LAB 4

MY FAVORITE COLOR

MATERIALS

- ▸ oil pastels
- ▸ watercolor paints
- ▸ colored pencils
- ▸ crayons
- ▸ card stock
- ▸ a container of water
- ▸ soft watercolor brushes
- ▸ newspaper
- ▸ colorful scrap paper
- ▸ scissors
- ▸ glue stick

WHAT DO YOU THINK?

Do you have a favorite color or a special palette (set) of colors? Do you always reach for one particular color first in your crayon/paint/paper box? Why do you like that color best? How does that color make you feel? We are going to make a drawing using your favorite color!

LET'S GO!

1. Begin by choosing a subject to draw. It can be your favorite *anything*—from animals to a still life composed of your favorite toys or an abstract doodle to your own backyard! Our student loves cats and

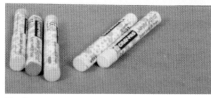

Fig. 1

Fig. 3

Fig. 5

Fig. 2

Fig. 4

Fig. 6

chose to draw a fantasy cat world. She also wanted to try making an abstract drawing, too! (Fig. 1.)

2. Gather your oil pastels, watercolor paints, colored pencils, and crayons. Choose all the shades and tints of your favorite color or palette so they are ready to use.

3. Use the oil pastels to create line drawings of your chosen subject. Do not fill in your card stock completely with the oil pastel to leave space for the watercolors. (Fig. 2.)

4. For the next layer, use the watercolors in the same color range as the pastels to fill in the remaining space on your paper. Let it dry. (Fig. 3.)

5. Look through your papers and choose some to cut up into the subject or details of what you have drawn! (Fig. 4.)

6. Glue the pieces onto your drawing and press hard for the glue to stick well! (Fig. 5.)

7. Add other details with colored pencils or crayons as you like. (Fig. 6.)

NIGHT CREATURES

MATERIALS

- ▸ images for reference, if desired
- ▸ card stock
- ▸ oil pastels
- ▸ watercolor or gouache paints
- ▸ soft watercolor brush
- ▸ water
- ▸ scissors
- ▸ dark-colored paper for the background
- ▸ chalk pastels
- ▸ clear glue

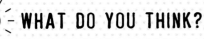

WHAT DO YOU THINK?

What do you see when you go outside at night? Have you noticed animals that only come out at night? What does the sky look like at night? Does your street or yard appear different at night? What is your favorite thing to do outside after dark? Do you have an idea now?

LET'S GO!

1. Choose your reference image to work from, if desired. Our student chose moths. (Fig. 1.)

2. Draw your creature images on the card stock with oil pastels using only lines, as you will also use watercolor paints to fill in the shapes. (Fig. 2.)

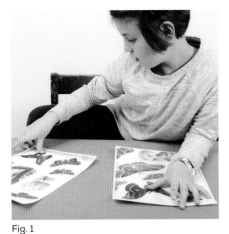
Fig. 1

Fig. 2

Fig. 3

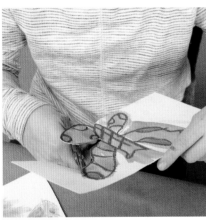
Fig. 4

Fig. 5

3. Use the watercolors and a wet brush to fill in the shapes of your night creatures. Let it dry. (Fig. 3.)

4. Cut out the creatures. (Fig. 4.)

5. Place them on your dark-colored background to decide where they might go. Save them for later. (Fig. 5.)

6. Using chalk pastels, draw your nighttime landscape on the dark-colored background. (Fig. 6.)

7. Apply clear glue to the back of the night creatures you drew and press them firmly onto the background. (Fig. 7.)

8. Add any other details, such as shiny foil stars or fuzzy stems, to your night scene as desired (optional).

Fig. 6

Fig. 7

STARS IN THE SKY

MATERIALS

- white paper
- pencil
- scissors
- black or dark-colored paper
- scrap paper
- glue stick
- white oil pastel
- ruler (optional)

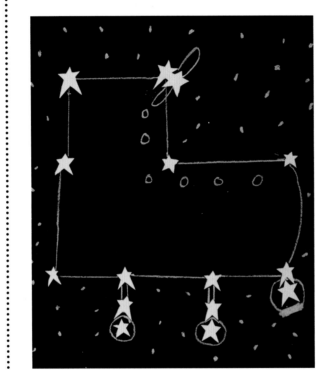

LET'S GO!

1. Draw out a few constellation ideas on your white paper with pencil. Keep the shapes simple! Our student chose a sport (roller skating) that she loves to do with her friends. Yours can be anything you can think up—from a favorite pet to a superhero or a special person or your favorite desert! (Fig. 1.)

2. Once you have your constellation idea drawn out, take a new piece of white paper and draw the stars that you will then cut out to make up your constellation. Draw as many as you need. Cut them out. (Fig. 2.)

3. Using your drawing as a reference, place the stars into formation on the dark night sky paper. (Fig. 3.)

 WHAT DO YOU THINK?

Do you ever look up at the night sky to find star constellations such as the Big Dipper or Southern Cross? What if you could make your own constellation? What would it be? Would it tell a story? Would you name the stars in the constellations?

Fig. 1

Fig. 2

Fig. 3

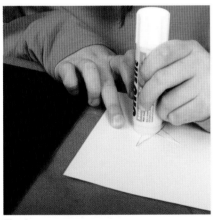

Fig. 4

Fig. 5

4. One by one, turn the stars upside-down on a piece of scrap paper and apply glue to the back. Press the stars into place on the dark paper. Continue until you've finished placing all the stars in your new constellation. (Figs. 4 and 5.)

5. Using the white oil pastel and a ruler (if you like), draw lines between the stars to finish expressing the shape of your constellation. (Fig. 6.)

6. Add more stars to your night sky with the oil pastel. (Fig. 7.) You can make a whole universe and write stories about your constellations!

Fig. 6

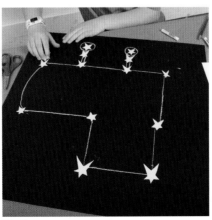

Fig. 7

COLLIDING CONTOURS

MATERIALS

▸ markers in various colors, including black
▸ paper

💡 WHAT DO YOU THINK?

Doodling with markers can be a fun way to create art. This lesson combines markers, contour drawing, and a little bit of imagination in a standard doodle. Look around your house and find some familiar objects, pets, or even people to use as subjects for your drawing. There is no limit to what you can choose to draw in this lesson!

Fig. 1

Fig. 2

Fig. 3

Fig. 4

LET'S GO!

1. Arrange your subject matter in front of you.

2. Start with a black marker and draw the first object's outline. This is called a *contour drawing*. (Fig. 1.)

3. As you begin drawing the next objects, slightly overlap them on top of one another creating new shapes. Continue drawing, repeating the shapes as desired to fill your paper. (Fig. 2.)

4. When you are satisfied with your drawing, add some color. Choose as many or as few colors as you wish. (Fig. 3.)

5. Color all the shapes you created with the markers. (Fig. 4.)

REPEAT YOURSELF

MATERIALS

▸ paper
▸ soft pastels
▸ object about the size of your hand
▸ damp paper towel

WHAT DO YOU THINK?

Repeating a drawing is good practice and improves your skills. Starting with one object is a simple way to practice. Using soft pastels, keep your marks bold and move forward without erasing. Choose an object to draw that appeals to you and that you haven't drawn before.

Fig. 1

Fig. 2

Fig. 3

Fig. 4

Fig. 5

LET'S GO!

1. Begin in the middle area of your paper. Using the soft pastels, draw the object at about its original size. (Fig. 1.)

2. Smudge the pastels with your finger to blend the colors. (Fig. 2.) Use a damp paper towel to remove the color from your fingers. (Fig. 3.)

3. Draw the object again, but now at only half its size. Decide where it will be placed on the paper. (Fig. 4.)

4. Continue to fill the paper with the original object, varying the size each time you draw it. (Fig. 5.)

MAP OF MY WORLD

MATERIALS

- ▸ oversized paper
- ▸ pencil
- ▸ eraser
- ▸ colored pencils
- ▸ colored markers
- ▸ crayons
- ▸ watercolor paints
- ▸ container of water
- ▸ soft watercolor brush

WHAT DO YOU THINK?

Have you ever used a paper map to find a special place? Have you ever read a book that has a map inside the pages to illustrate where things are located in the story? Think for a moment about your own world—the places you go and the special routes you take to get there. What do you see along the way? Making a map of your world is a wonderful way to express what is important to you. Sketch out some places you would like to include on your map. A written list of all the destinations will be useful, too!

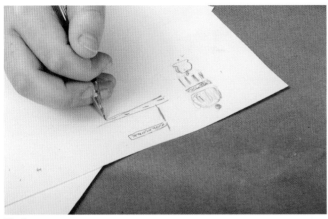
Fig. 1

Fig. 2

Fig. 3

Fig. 4

LET'S GO!

1. Start your map in the middle or one corner of the paper so you have room for all your destinations. Begin to draw lightly with a pencil so you are able to erase, if needed. Add color when your ideas are complete. (Figs. 1 and 2.)

2. Add words, if you like, to name your special places. (Fig. 3.)

3. Use watercolor paints to easily add color to large areas. (Fig. 4.)

STILL LIFE—TWISTED

MATERIALS

- objects for a still life
- pencil
- card stock
- colored pencils
- watercolor paints
- container of water
- soft watercolor brush

WHAT DO YOU THINK?

Surreal art is a combination of things you might not expect to see together. For this lesson, the still life you choose will have a strange combination of objects. Our student chose a toy giraffe, a bottle with a flower, and some fruit. This is a starting point for our student to create a bizarre, dream-like subject for his drawing! What will you choose? Will you tell a story through your drawing?

Fig. 1

Fig. 2

LET'S GO!

1. Begin by arranging your objects in front of you.

2. Draw the objects with a pencil on the card stock paper. (Fig. 1.)

3. Using your imagination, and perhaps remembering a dream or story, add some details to your drawing. When you are finished with the details, add color to the drawing. (Fig. 2.)

4. In larger areas or to create a different effect, use watercolor paint. Let it dry. (Fig. 3.)

Fig. 3

EXPRESS YOURSELF WITH PAINTING

*"Painting from nature is not copying the object;
it is realizing one's sensations."*
—PAUL CÉZANNE

I believe there is a universal love for painting. To push paint around with a brush or other tool is a satisfying act. These labs explore working with ink, watercolor, and acrylic paints in small and large sizes. Deeply exploring color and making personal decisions about the subject and composition of the paintings are often at the core of these lessons. These explorations nurture and allow self-expression to flourish and help develop a greater sense of self through the decision-making process.

FOLD ME A GARDEN

MATERIALS

- ▸ tempera paint in various colors
- ▸ paper plate
- ▸ water
- ▸ soft paintbrush
- ▸ paper
- ▸ newspaper

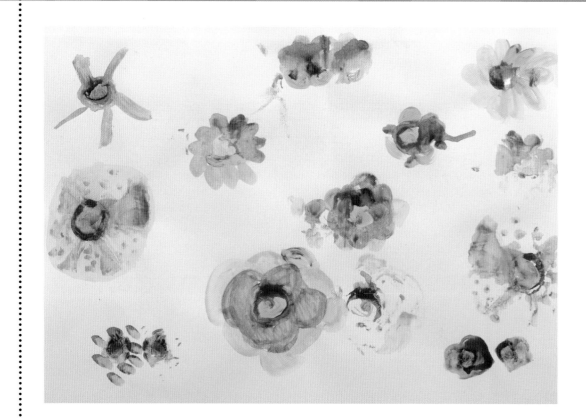

WHAT DO YOU THINK?

What are your favorite plants? Do you ever work in a garden, or walk through a garden? If you could plant a garden, what would your garden look like?

Fig. 1

Fig. 2

Fig. 3

Fig. 4

Fig. 5

LET'S GO!

1. To begin, dispense the paint colors onto the paper plate.

2. Using a wet paintbrush, choose your first color to create a plant on the left side of the newspaper. (Fig. 1.)

3. Working quickly, with a wet brush and plenty of paint, create your first plant in your garden.

4. When the first plant is done and still wet, fold the paper in half and rub the backside of the paper over the wet plant you just painted. The wet plant should print a new plant on the right side of the paper! (Fig. 2.)

5. Continue to "plant" your garden in this fashion until it is full of beautiful plants! (Figs. 3, 4, and 5.)

WHAT'S YOUR SUPERPOWER?

MATERIALS

- scrap paper
- pencil
- canvas panel or stretched canvas
- palette knife
- acrylic paints in various colors
- paper plate
- paintbrushes in various shapes and sizes
- container of water
- newspaper
- scissors
- colored paper in various colors
- pens in various colors
- glue stick

WHAT DO YOU THINK?

Have you ever dreamed of having a superpower? What would you use your superpower for? Would you use it to help someone? In this lesson, we use mixed media to create a painting that illustrates our super-power! You might even go further and write a short story on the back of the canvas about your adventures with your superpower. Our student chose invisibility and loves books, so a library was her preferred background.

Fig. 1

Fig. 2

Fig. 3

Fig. 4

Fig. 5

The collage paper pieces will go on top of the painting, so keep that in mind! (Fig. 1.)

2. Using your palette knife, mix any paint colors you may need on the paper plate, so you don't have to stop while you are painting. (Fig. 2.)

3. Paint in the entire background as you have sketched it, but feel free to make changes as you go! It is part of the process to evaluate as you create and change your mind. Let the background dry, then paint your foreground. Wash your brush between colors. Let the paint dry. (Fig. 3.)

4. Draw and cut out the colored paper pieces for the collage elements of your illustration. Add details with pens and paint. (Fig. 4.)

5. Using the glue stick, glue the collage elements onto your painted background. (Fig. 5.)

LET'S GO!

1. First, sketch a few super-power ideas with your pencil on scrap paper. Now choose your favorite to sketch on your canvas. Think about what the background and setting for your illustration will be. Decide what you want to paint and which parts will include a cut paper collage.

STRIPES AND LINES

MATERIALS

- ▸ acrylic paint in various colors
- ▸ oil pastels
- ▸ ruler
- ▸ canvas
- ▸ paper plate
- ▸ paintbrushes in various shapes and sizes
- ▸ container of water
- ▸ newspaper

WHAT DO YOU THINK?

Do you think you could express a feeling or idea in a painting using just straight lines or color—or both? This lesson challenges you to create an abstract painting with those rules! Our student expressed the feeling of movement and warm weather—skateboarding in summer!

Fig. 1

Fig. 2

Fig. 3

Fig. 4

LET'S GO!

1. Choose the paint colors you want to work with to express your feeling or idea.

2. Using oil pastels, create straight lines on the canvas. Use a ruler, if you like. Our student chose all horizontal lines, but you can make them any way your idea takes them! The lines can overlap, cross other lines, form shapes, or be floating inside the boundaries of the canvas. (Fig. 1.)

3. Dispense the paint colors onto the paper plate. Begin painting between the lines you have drawn. (Fig. 2.)

4. Continue painting until all the canvas is covered. Let it dry. (Fig. 3.)

5. When the paint is dry, use the oil pastels to make the lines you drew bolder. (Fig. 4.)

COLOR ME HAPPY

MATERIALS

- acrylic paint in various colors including black and white
- paper plate
- small foam paint roller
- large canvas
- spray bottle of water
- pushpin
- 2 friends
- flashlight
- pencil
- paintbrushes
- container of water

LET'S GO!

1. Choose your colors, plus white for the background, based on the mood you want to express. Dispense them onto the paper plate. (Fig. 1.)

2. Pick up the colors with the foam paint roller. Begin rolling and mixing the paint right on the canvas. Cover the whole canvas with your colorful mood! (Figs. 2 and 3.)

3. Squirt some water from the spray bottle onto the wet paint for a different texture. Let it dry. Add more paint with the roller, if you like. Let it dry again. (Fig. 4.)

WHAT DO YOU THINK?

What color makes you feel happy? Is there more than one? Colors in paintings can express a mood or feeling. You will choose some colors to represent the mood of this painting and let them do the talking. Your silhouette will be the subject of your painting.

Fig. 1

Fig. 2

Fig. 3

Fig. 4

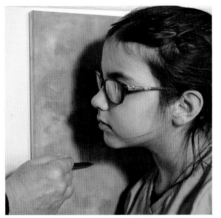
Fig. 5

4. Sit in a chair with your shoulder touching the wall. Hang your canvas on the wall with a pushpin as shown. Have one friend shine a flashlight toward you to create a shadow. A task lamp will also work. Ask another friend to trace your profile with a pencil on the canvas, (Fig. 5.)

5. Go around the pencil line with a brush and the black paint. Paint all the space inside the line black—or mix it up and paint the outside space black! Try it both ways for a pair of paintings! (Figs. 6 and 7.)

Fig. 6

Fig. 7

BLACK AND WHITE

MATERIALS

- a colorful artwork that you made
- pencil
- stretched canvas
- acrylic paint in white and black
- paper plate
- paintbrushes in various sizes
- newspaper
- container of water

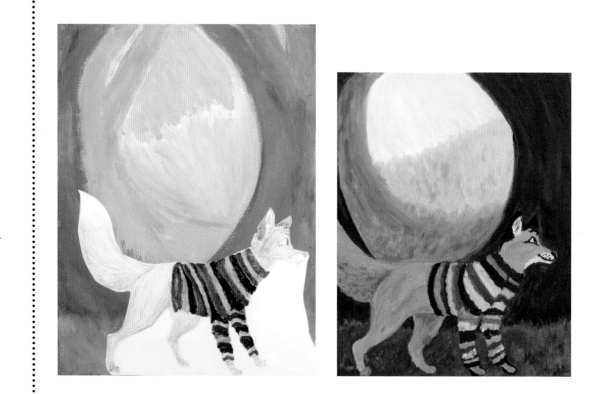

WHAT DO YOU THINK?

Have you ever tried to make a painting using only black and white paint? In this lesson, we will copy a painting that you have made in color and turn it into a black and white painting. The process is fun and helps train your eye to see how light or dark a color is—known as *value*.

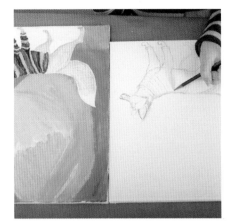

Fig. 1

Fig. 2

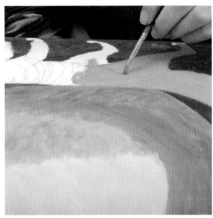

Fig. 3

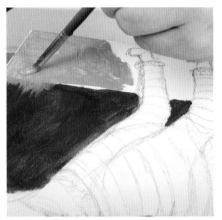

Fig. 4

Fig. 5

Fig. 6

LET'S GO!

1. Examine your colorful original artwork. Now draw it using a pencil on your new canvas. (Fig. 1.)

2. Dispense some white and black paint onto your paper plate. Combine the colors so you have three or four light grays and three or four darker grays.

3. Look at your colorful artwork and decide where the lightest parts are. Paint the lightest portions on your new painting with the lightest gray paint. (Fig. 2.)

4. Continue examining the colors, deciding which parts are the next darkest shade of gray. Paint those parts next. (Fig. 3.)

5. Continue going through the colors selecting the progression of darker shades of gray. If needed, adjust your gray shades on the palette. (Fig. 4.)

6. If you want to adjust a shade of gray on your painting, wait until the first layer is dry then paint over the top of the shade, making it either lighter or darker. (Figs. 5 and 6.)

COLOR POPS

MATERIALS

- paper
- pencil
- acrylic paints in various colors including white and black
- paper plate
- paintbrushes in various sizes
- container of water
- stretched canvas
- newspaper

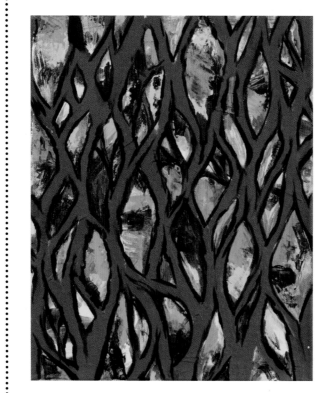

LET'S GO!

1. Using paper and pencil, sketch out a few ideas for the foreground—the pattern of branches or a pattern of anything with holes or spaces in it! (Fig. 1.)

WHAT DO YOU THINK?

Have you ever looked up through a tree to see the bright blue sky between the pattern of branches? It can form a natural yet abstract pattern; windowpanes and fences can do this, too. Can you think of other settings like this? In this lesson, we will create a foreground pattern in shades of gray over a background of beautiful color.

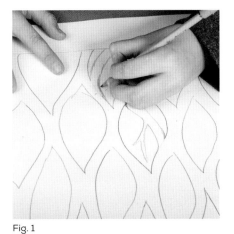
Fig. 1

Fig. 2

Fig. 3

Fig. 4

Fig. 5

Fig. 6

2. Choose the colors you want to use for the background and dispense them onto the paper plate palette. (Fig. 2.)

3. Decide how your brush-strokes should look on the canvas. You may test them on paper first or just go for it on the canvas. Remember, you can always paint over anything you don't like in your next layer once the first layer is dry. (Fig. 3.)

4. Cover the entire canvas with your marks, making as many layers as desired. Let it dry. (Fig. 3.)

5. With a pencil, draw the fore-ground pattern you designed on top of your colored layer. (Fig. 4.)

6. Using the white and black paints, mix up a few shades of gray. Use these to paint in your pattern covering the pencil lines. (Fig. 5.)

7. Add different shades of gray from very light to dark to create contrast and depth in your painting. (Fig. 6.)

AROUND THE COLOR WHEEL

MATERIALS

▸ pencil
▸ a compass or circular objects to trace
▸ watercolor paper
▸ ruler
▸ 2 containers of water (1 for wetting paintbrushes, 1 for washing paintbrushes)
▸ soft watercolor brush
▸ watercolor paints
▸ scrap paper

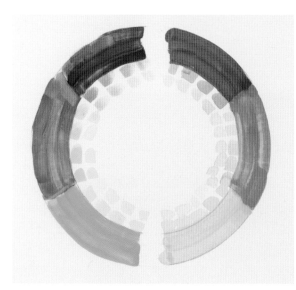

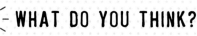 ## WHAT DO YOU THINK?

This lesson shows you how to mix colors using watercolors to create new colors. It is helpful to have a chart showing you how to get the colors you are looking for. If you make it yourself, it is even better! This is a great tool to make and keep!

LET'S GO!

1. With a pencil and compass or round object, draw the largest circle you can on the watercolor paper. (Fig. 1.)

2. Draw a smaller circle inside the larger circle, leaving space between to paint in. Using a ruler and pencil, evenly divide the space beween the circles into six wedges. (Fig. 2.)

3. You should have two containers of water—one for wetting clean brushes and one for washing dirty brushes. Wet your brush and start by painting in the red color on the top of one of the six wedges. Wash your brush thoroughly in the wash water. Skip a wedge to the right of the red and paint a yellow wedge in the same fashion. (Fig. 3.)

Fig. 1

Fig. 2

Fig. 3

Fig. 4

Fig. 5

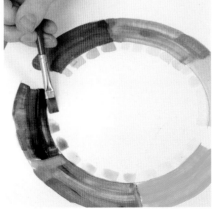

Fig. 6

4. Use the lid of your paint box to mix yellow and red paints together to make your first new color—orange! Paint the new color into the wedge between the red and yellow wedges. (Fig. 4.)

5. Wash your brush. Now paint blue into the wedge directly across from the orange. Finish the remaining two wedges by mixing as you did in step 4, but this time mix blue with red and then blue with yellow. (Fig. 5.)

6. Your wheel now has the three primary colors—red, yellow, and blue as well as the three secondary (mixed) colors of orange, purple, and green. With watercolor it's easy to make each of these colors lighter by simply adding water to the colors on the lid of your paint box. Try this yourself! First, use scrap paper to check your colors if you're unsure, then paint a mark under each original color on the inside of the ring. See how many you different colors you can make! (Fig. 6.)

LAB 18

FANTASY WATERCOLOR GARDENS

MATERIALS

- ▸ masking tape
- ▸ watercolor paper
- ▸ foam core board
- ▸ watercolor paints
- ▸ watercolor brushes with round and flat profiles
- ▸ 2 containers of water (1 for wetting paintbrushes, 1 for washing paintbrushes)

LET'S GO!

1. Using the masking tape, attach the paper around all four sides to the foam core board. This keeps the paper flat while it is wet and allows it to dry flat, too. (Fig. 1.)

2. Mix some colors for your flowers in the lid of your paint box. Mix some stem and leaf colors, too! Use one water container to wash your brushes and one container to wet your paints. This keeps your paint colors from getting muddy. (Fig. 2.)

WHAT DO YOU THINK?

Have you ever examined flowers closely? Look in a garden, a park, books or magazines for flowers and leaves. Did you notice what shapes the different petals, leaves, and stems have? In this lesson, we look closely at the shapes we can make with our brushes and create our very own fantasy garden filled with flowers you paint.

Fig. 1

Fig. 2

Fig. 3

Fig. 4

Fig. 5

Fig. 6

3. Dip your brush into the clean water and paint a stem with leaves with just the water on your paper. Do you like the shape you made? If not, let it dry and try again. If you are satisfied, just paint over the wet shape with your choice of color. (Fig. 3.)

4. Continue experimenting with water only and then add color into the wet shapes. Let the color flow in and try to brush over it only once. If you don't want the colors to flow and mix, simply let them dry and they will layer easily. (Fig. 4.)

5. Try all your different-shaped brushes to make many dif-ferent leaf and petal shapes. Push down on the brush and pull toward you to create a petal form. Turn your entire painting around to create the petal shapes you desire. (Fig. 5.)

6. Add flower centers and other details you choose to make your garden bloom! (Fig. 6.)

BIG TIME CANVAS

MATERIALS

▸ pencil
▸ scrap paper
▸ acrylic paints in various colors
▸ large piece of canvas, wood, or cardboard, primed with gesso
▸ foam paint rollers
▸ chalk
▸ damp paper towels
▸ paintbrushes in various shapes and sizes
▸ paper plate
▸ newspaper

WHAT DO YOU THINK?

Have you ever wondered what it would be like to paint a very large painting of something very small? It's exciting to do! If you have a large piece of canvas, wood, or even cardboard, I encourage you to try this lesson. Think of a few small things that would be fun to paint very large then choose your favorite one to feature in this painting.

LET'S GO!

1. First, sketch out some of your ideas with pencil on scrap paper. Choose your favorite for the painting. (Fig. 1.)

2. Choose the colors for your background. Keep in mind which colors will be used

Fig. 1

Fig. 2

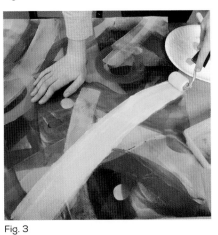
Fig. 3

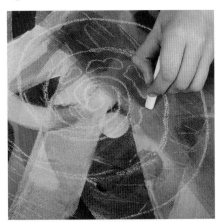
Fig. 4

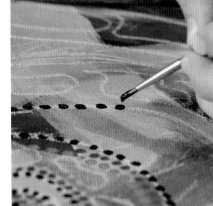
Fig. 5

Fig. 6

for your subject in the foreground. Paint the background first to cover the entire canvas. Use the paint roller to apply the colors one at a time. If you want the colors to blend, do not wait for each layer to dry. If you do not want them to blend, let them dry between colors. Wash roller in sink between colors and squeeze out excess water. (Fig. 2.)

3. Layer as many background colors as you like. Let them dry. (Fig. 3.)

4. Using the chalk, draw your subject on the canvas. Remember to go as large as the canvas will allow! If you need to erase a mark, just use a damp paper towel. (Fig. 4.)

5. Begin painting your subject on top of the chalk lines. (Fig. 5.)

6. Fill in the subject with colors you like. Our student decided to use mostly black and white with dots, but you should choose what you think is best for your painting. (Fig. 6.)

FORESTS AND TREES

MATERIALS

- acrylic paints in various colors
- paintbrushes in various shapes and sizes
- stretched canvas or panel
- container of water
- india ink
- newspaper
- drinking straw

WHAT DO YOU THINK?

Do you ever draw or paint trees? Do you have a favorite tree near where you live? Trees are home to many birds and animals as well as insects. Some trees live hundreds of years! Have you planted a tree? Trees are very important plants for our planet! This lesson is all about painting imaginary trees and the places where they live.

LET'S GO!

1. First, choose a time of day and a season of the year for your tree to live in. Is it a sunny day or rainy? What time of day is it? Choose the colors that best represent your idea.

Fig. 1

Fig. 2

Fig. 3

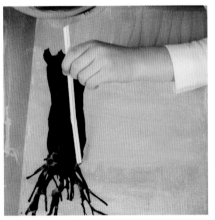

Fig. 4

2. Paint the entire canvas with your chosen sky and land colors. Make sure your sky meets the land and the whole canvas is covered. Let it dry. (Fig. 1.)

3. Using a small paintbrush and the india ink, paint your first tree trunk on your canvas. Leave a little puddle at the top of the trunk. Put your brush down on the newspaper to keep it ready to use again. (Fig. 2.)

4. Position the straw close to the puddle of ink you left at the top of the trunk and blow short bursts of air through it to form ink branches. You can follow the droplets with air through your straw to make long branches! Keep your lips tight around the straw so all the air goes through the straw. Take a break between blows so you don't get dizzy! (Fig. 3.)

5. Keep going until you have all the branches you want. Add more ink to the puddle, if needed. Make a few trees or a whole forest! (Fig. 4.)

UNIT 4

EXPRESS YOURSELF WITH PRINTMAKING

"I just decided, when someone says you can't do something, DO MORE OF IT."
—FAITH RINGGOLD

Printmaking is a favorite medium in our classroom. From the excitement of revealing what a hand-carved stamp will look like to making your own texture plate tool to use in future art, there is always a thrill within the process.

This chapter explores a variety of types of printmaking to introduce the concept of making multiples in different ways. Each art print will reflect a series of choices and, then, self-expression through these choices. The printmaking chapter includes simple rubbing (frottage) prints, foam prints, carved soft-cut prints, stencils, string prints, shaving cream prints, and monoprints. The repetitive "making" process of printmaking allows freedom of expression, risk taking, and intuitive exploration.

LAB 21

MUSIC-INSPIRED STRING PRINTS

MATERIALS

- ▸ a music source
- ▸ cardboard square
- ▸ pencil
- ▸ clear glue
- ▸ scissors
- ▸ cotton string
- ▸ brayer
- ▸ Plexiglas sheet
- ▸ water-based block printing ink in 2 colors
- ▸ white paper
- ▸ newspaper

💡 WHAT DO YOU THINK?

When you hear music playing does it make you feel a particular way—energetic, sad, jumpy, or sleepy? Turn on some music and think about the feelings you get from what you hear. How do you feel? Close your eyes and imagine the colors and shapes or lines that you think go with the music. What are they? Try drawing with your finger in the air along with the music. What kind or lines did you draw? Let's take those answers and make some *ekphrastic art*—that is, art inspired by another art form!

Fig. 1

Fig. 2

Fig. 3

Fig. 4

Fig. 5

3. Cut string to the lengths of the glue lines and press them into the glue lines on the cardboard. Let dry overnight. This is your printing plate. (Fig. 1.)

4. Using the brayer, roll out a small spoonful of a lighter-color ink on the Plexiglas sheet until smooth. (Fig. 2.)

5. Roll the ink from the brayer onto your printing plate, coating just the string completely. You are ready to print! (Fig. 3.)

6. Place the paper on top of the printing plate. Hold it in place while rubbing it with your fingertips to contact all the string. (Fig. 4.)

7. You can also use a spoon to rub the paper if it's easier. (Fig. 5.)

8. Peel the paper off to see your print! Decide where the next print will go and repeat with the same ink color until finished, then switch to a darker-color ink (no need to wash in between, just roll the excess ink onto the newspaper).

LET'S GO!

1. On the cardboard, draw your lines and shapes with a pencil. Listen to the music again to remember the shapes and lines.

2. Squeeze the glue over the lines making a thick bead of glue as you go.

WORD UP

MATERIALS

- pencil
- card stock
- single hole punch
- scissors
- tape
- paper
- acrylic paint
- paper plate
- sponge brush
- 2 pieces of firm cardboard for storing your stencil

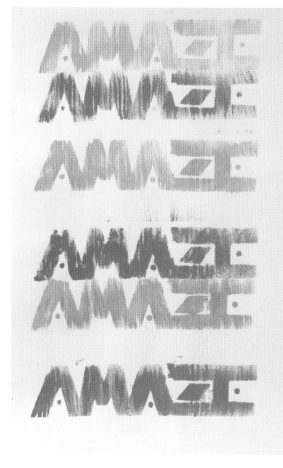

WHAT DO YOU THINK?

There are many artists who use words in their art to express a message or idea. Which word means something to you—right now—today? Choose a single word that really shows how you feel, an uplifting thought or a message you want to tell everyone.

Fig. 1

Fig. 2

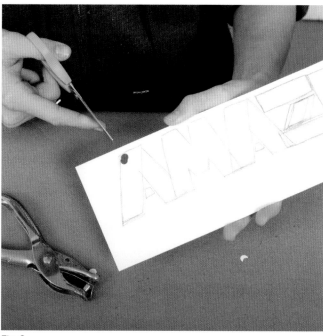

Fig. 3

LET'S GO!

1. Beginning 1 inch (2.5 cm) from the top and sides, use a pencil to draw block letters of your word on the card stock. You can look at different fonts and letter styles in books or computers or simply make up your own! (Fig. 1.)

2. Using the hole punch, make a hole inside the first letter. This will give you a starting point to cut out your letters. (Fig. 2.)

3. Insert the scissors into the hole and cut away the inside of the block letters you drew. (Fig. 3.)

(continued)

Fig. 4

Fig. 5

Fig. 6

4. Trim stencil to have at least 1 inch (2.5 cm) around the word. (Fig. 4.) Using masking tape, affix the stencil to the paper you are going to print on. Think about how many times you will print it and where the print will go. (Fig. 5.)

5. Dispense a small amount of paint on your paper plate. Lightly dab the foam brush in the paint and then onto the paper plate to distribute the paint evenly on the brush. (Fig. 6.)

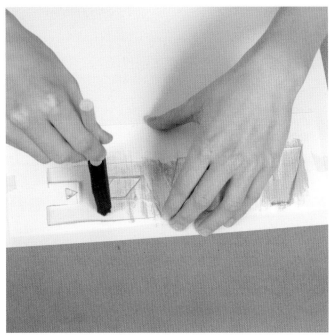

Fig. 7

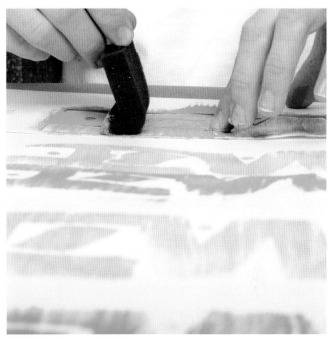

Fig. 8

Fig. 9

6. Gently dab the foam brush up and down onto the stencil. Continue across the word as you did for the first letter. Bounce it up and down and not under the stencil's edges. Be gentle! (Fig. 7.)

7. If you like, change colors as you move your stencil to print your word again. (Fig. 8.)

8. Remember to handle your stencil gently when it's wet. After it dries, store it between two pieces of firm cardboard if you want to save it for another project. (Fig. 9.)

LAB 23

TEXTURE PLATES

MATERIALS

- ▸ clear or masking tape
- ▸ scrap mat boards
- ▸ large sequins
- ▸ clear glue
- ▸ net bag from produce
- ▸ paper clips
- ▸ crayons
- ▸ watercolor paints
- ▸ watercolor paintbrush
- ▸ container of water
- ▸ paper

WHAT DO YOU THINK?

Do you ever notice a photo of a cat can look furry while still being a smooth photograph? This is called *visual texture*. This lesson is a tool-making lesson that will help you create visual texture. Making your own tools for creating art is a very personal way to express your ideas. Keep an eye out for other interesting things that you could turn into texture plates.

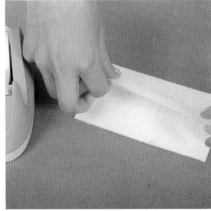

Fig. 1

Fig. 2

Fig. 3

Fig. 4

Fig. 5

LET'S GO!

1. For the tape plate, attach various lengths of tape in the sizes you desire onto the mat board. (Fig. 1.)

2. On another mat board, arrange the large sequins as you like and glue them in place. (Fig. 2.)

3. Cut the net bag to fit on a different mat board and glue it in place. (Fig. 3.)

4. Arrange the paper clips, in any way you like, on another mat board and glue them in place. (Fig. 4.) Let all the items with glue to dry for several hours or overnight.

5. Create a drawing using the texture plates. Place a piece of paper over one of the textures you made and then rub the paper with the side of a crayon (paper wrapper removed) revealing the texture underneath. Add watercolor paint over the crayon for additional color. (Fig. 5.) Keep making more texture plates to use in your future artwork!

BIG ROLLING PRINTS

MATERIALS

▸ pencil
▸ adhesive-backed craft foam
▸ scissors
▸ ballpoint pen
▸ large plastic container or #10 can, may be obtained from a school cafeteria or a local restaurant
▸ ink pads with raised foam pad
▸ brayer
▸ water-based block printing ink
▸ large sheets of paper to print on
▸ Plexiglas sheet

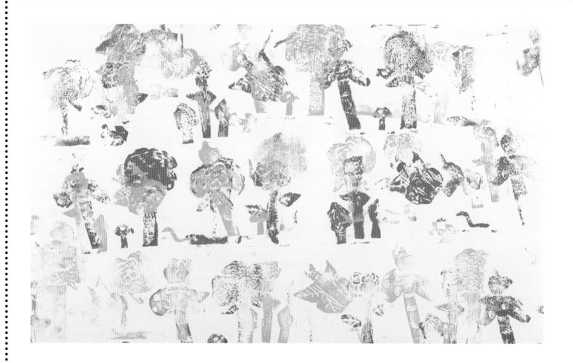

WHAT DO YOU THINK?

Printmaking is an art form that often produces multiples of the same design using a printing plate. In this lesson, we will make a big rolling printing plate that can print a large piece of paper easily. Think about what you would like to create over and over again in a BIG way.

Remember, if you choose words, you must create a mirrored (reversed) image to have them print properly.

Fig. 1

Fig. 2

Fig. 3

LET'S GO!

1. With a pencil, draw your designs on the **paper side** of the foam. (Fig. 1.)

2. Cut out the designs with scissors. (Fig. 2.)

3. Add details to the designs with a ballpoint pen on the **foam side**. Press hard to indent the foam. You should be able to feel the lines in the foam. (Fig. 3.)

(continued)

Fig. 4

Fig. 5

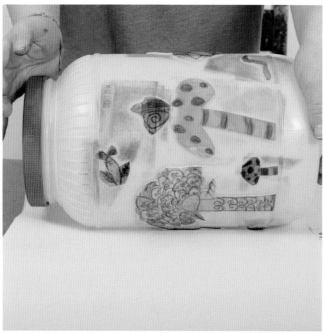

Fig. 6

4. Peel off the backing on each design and stick them onto the sides of the container, pressing hard to adhere. (Fig. 4.)

5. Test the printing plate using the ink pads to apply the ink directly to the designs in a rocking motion. Ink all the designs before rolling. (Fig. 5.)

6. Press your inked design onto the paper, pressing hard to print. This first print is called the *artist proof*. (Fig. 6.) Check your proof and decide if you need to add more details or designs.

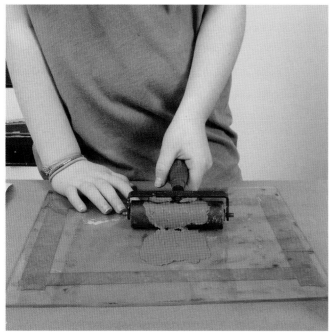

Fig. 7

Fig. 8

Fig. 9

7. Using the brayer, roll out some printmaking ink on the Plexiglas sheet until the ink is smooth. (Fig. 7.)

8. Roll the ink from the brayer onto the designs. Don't add too much ink or you will lose details of the design that you drew with the ballpoint pen. (Fig. 8.)

9. Roll the printing plate onto another sheet of paper, pressing firmly. Let it dry. (Fig. 9.)

SIMPLE PRINTS

MATERIALS

▸ pencil
▸ paper
▸ card stock
▸ scissors
▸ glue stick
▸ crayons

WHAT DO YOU THINK?

You don't always need a lot of supplies to create a really exciting print, just an idea and a few pieces of paper. For this lesson, the subjects are repeated over and over in the composition. Our student chose one tree to repeat, but you can choose several different items to create your own artwork!

Fig. 1

Fig. 2

Fig. 3

Fig. 4

Fig. 5

LET'S GO!

1. First, sketch some of your ideas with pencil on paper. Your print will most prominently show the outline or contour. Choose the ideas you like best and draw them on the cardstock. (Fig. 1.)

2. Cut out the contour drawing with scissors. Repeat this for all of the drawings you want to use in your artwork. (Fig. 2.)

3. Glue the cut-out drawing to another piece of cardstock with the glue stick and press firmly. Do this with all of your cut-out drawings. (Fig. 3.)

4. Now you are ready to print! Position your cut-out drawing under the paper where you want it to be printed. (Fig. 4.) Rub with the side of a crayon (paper wrapper removed) until you see your image appear.

5. Reposition your cut-out drawing and repeat as many times as desired. Do this with all of the cut-out drawings you created. (Fig. 5.)

MATERIALS

▸ acrylic paints in various colors including black
▸ paper plate
▸ paintbrushes in various shapes and sizes
▸ container of water
▸ quart-size (1.1 L) plastic bags
▸ paper
▸ newspaper
▸ photocopy of a picture of yourself
▸ permanent marker

WHAT DO YOU THINK?

Everyone takes selfies now, but self-portraits have been around for hundreds of years. For this lesson, we will create some pop art self-portraits expressing your feelings captured in a selfie. Choose your photo and decide, through color choice and background design, what you want to express.

Fig. 1

Fig. 2

Fig. 3

Fig. 4

Fig. 5

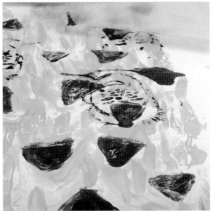

Fig. 6

LET'S GO!

1. Dispense some paint for background colors onto the paper plate. Using a *very* wet paintbrush, quickly paint patterns you like in your chosen colors onto the plastic bag. (Fig. 1.)

2. Flip the bag paint-side down on top of your paper and smooth firmly to print. (Fig. 2.) Repeat to fill your background as desired.

3. Place your photocopied picture under another plastic bag and use the permanent marker to trace your portrait onto the bag. (Figs. 3 and 4.)

4. Flip the bag over. Using black paint and a *very* wet paint-brush, quickly trace over the marker lines on the back of the bag. Immediately press the black paint on the plastic bag firmly onto your background to print your portrait. (Fig. 5.)

5. Peel up the bag and repeat as much as desired over your background. (Fig. 6.)

TAPE STENCIL T-SHIRT

MATERIALS

- ▸ foam core
- ▸ plain white t-shirt
- ▸ tape
- ▸ acrylic paint in various colors
- ▸ textile medium, such as chromacryl
- ▸ paper plate
- ▸ paintbrushes in various shapes and sizes
- ▸ container of water

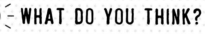

LET'S GO!

1. Put the foam core inside the T-shirt to create a firm flat surface to paint on and keep the paint off the back of the shirt. Smooth any wrinkles with your hands. (Fig. 1.)

2. Apply the tape to the T-shirt to create your pattern. Press the tape firmly to the shirt. The tape will leave white lines where it is placed. (Fig. 2.)

WHAT DO YOU THINK?

Would you like to create some art to wear or make some for others to wear? This is one of three lessons that will help you get your art and ideas on T-shirts! This one uses tape as a stencil. Think of some ideas for colors you want to use and the image you want to create with the tape creating the lines. Try it out on paper first, if you like!

Fig. 1

Fig. 2

Fig. 3

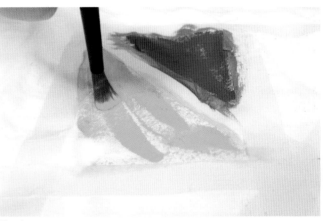

Fig. 4

Fig. 5

3. Dispense the paint onto the paper plate and add few drops of textile medium to each color. Begin painting between the taped areas. (Fig. 3.)

4. Fill in all the areas with color and let the paint dry. (Fig. 4.)

5. Once dry, remove the tape. Follow the manufacturer's directions for setting the textile medium. (Fig. 5.)

BLOCK-PRINTED T-SHIRT

MATERIALS

- ▸ pencil
- ▸ paper
- ▸ soft-cut lino block
- ▸ lino cutter
- ▸ adult to supervise the cutting
- ▸ ink pad
- ▸ scrap wood to mount block (optional)
- ▸ contact glue, to be used by an adult
- ▸ foam core board
- ▸ plain white T-shirt
- ▸ brayer
- ▸ fabric block printing ink or fabric paint
- ▸ Plexiglas sheet

WHAT DO YOU THINK?

Creating your own carved stamp or block is exciting as you can use it for many art projects. We suggest using cutters that come with a pen-like handle and soft-cut lino blocks for safety and ease of use. Your block can be any design you can draw and carve. Don't overlook the simpler designs that can be rotated to form more complex designs when printed. Our student achieved this with a triangle, rotating the block to print it pointing up and down! Remember to think about what represents *you* in a design.

Fig. 1

Fig. 2

LET'S GO!

1. Draw out a few ideas with pencil on paper. For a line to print it must be raised on the block, meaning that you will carve away the *negative space* or what is *not* the line. An easy way to see this as you are drawing is to make a double line for every line you draw. If your design is a solid filled-in shape, you will carve away everything around the outside of the shape. (Fig. 1.)

2. Draw your design with pencil on the lino block. Color in the negative space you will carve away, if desired. (Fig. 2.)

(continued)

Fig. 3

Fig. 4

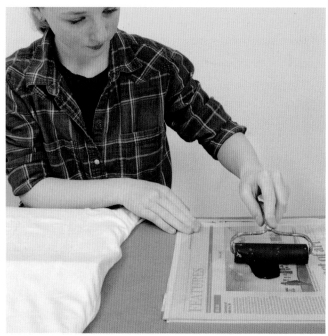

Fig. 5

3. Hold the lino cutter as shown. With an adult supervising, begin carving, keeping your other hand behind the path of the tool. **Never carve toward yourself.** Rotate the block as needed so you always carve away from yourself. (Fig. 3.)

4. When your carving is complete, test your block with the ink pad and paper. We attached the block to a piece of wood with contact glue (to be used by an adult), as the stamp was large, but this is optional. Test the block on paper to see how it prints. Do you need to carve anything else away? Also test out how many prints you will create on the shirt. (Fig. 4.)

5. Put the foam core inside the shirt to form a smooth printing surface on the shirt and to keep the ink from leaking through to the back of the shirt. Using the brayer, roll out the printing ink onto the Plexiglas sheet until smooth. (Fig. 5.)

Fig. 6

Fig. 7

Fig. 8

6. Using the brayer, apply the ink to the block in two different directions to cover the design. (Fig. 6.)

7. Begin printing at the top and work your way down the shirt. Each time you print, reapply the ink with the brayer. Using too much ink will produce a less crisp print, so don't over-do the ink. Press hard on the block when printing! (Fig. 7.)

8. Wash and dry your brayer, Plexiglas, and block thoroughly to change ink colors or to store your tools. Print the second color just like you did the first. Let everything dry overnight. Follow the ink manufacturer's directions for setting the ink for washing. (Fig. 8.)

BOOKPLATES

MATERIALS

- soft-cut lino block
- pencil
- paper
- adult to supervise the cutting
- lino cutter
- ink pad
- scrap wood to mount block (optional)
- contact glue, to be used by an adult
- baby wipes
- brayer
- water-based block printing ink
- Plexiglas sheet
- newspapers
- scissors
- glue stick

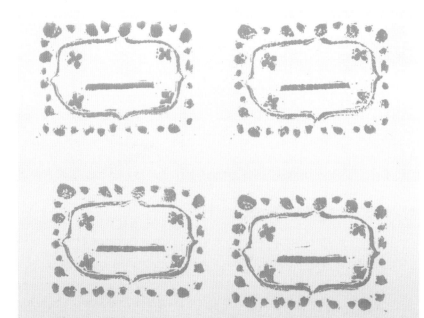

WHAT DO YOU THINK?

A book is a treasured belonging and something wonderful to share with a friend. To help keep your books returning to your personal library, you can make your very own block-printed bookplate. Bookplates are glued into the front of a book and identify the owner. In this lesson, you'll create a fine art print by carving a block into a stamp you can use over and over to identify your books.

Fig. 1

Fig. 2

Fig. 3

LET'S GO!

1. Begin by tracing around your block for size. Draw a few ideas for your design with pencil on paper. For a line to print it must be raised on the block, meaning you will carve away the *negative space* or what is *not* the line. An easy way to see this as you are drawing is to make a double line for every line you draw. If your design is a solid filled-in shape you will carve away everything around the outside of the shape. Leave a space or make a line in the design to sign your name. (Figs. 1 and 2.)

2. Draw your design with pencil on the block. Color in the negative space that you will carve away, if desired. (Fig. 3.)

(continued)

Fig. 4

Fig. 5

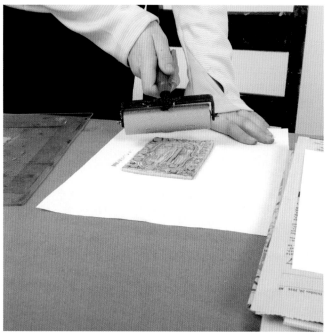

Fig. 6

3. Hold the lino cutter as shown. With an adult supervising, begin carving, keeping your other hand behind the path of the tool. **Never carve toward yourself.** Rotate the block as needed so you always carve away from yourself. (Fig. 4.)

4. When your carving is complete test your block with the ink pad and paper. We glued the block to a piece of wood, as the stamp was large, but this is optional. Test the block to see how it prints. Do you need to carve anything else away? (Fig. 5.)

5. Wipe the ink off the block with a baby wipe. Roll out the ink with the brayer until smooth. Using the brayer, apply the ink to the block in two different directions to cover the design. (Fig. 6.)

Fig. 7

Fig. 8

6. Place your paper on top of the newspaper. Position your block and then firmly press it down onto the paper. (Fig. 7.)

7. Repeat to fill the paper with prints. Re-ink the block each time. Let everything dry and cut out your new bookplate. Glue them into your books with a glue stick! (Fig. 8.) Don't forget to sign your name!

SWIRLY PRINTS

MATERIALS

- ▸ shaving cream
- ▸ plastic tray or old baking sheet
- ▸ card stock
- ▸ plastic scraper cut from a discarded container lid
- ▸ craft paint in various colors
- ▸ paper plate
- ▸ container of water
- ▸ paintbrush
- ▸ plastic fork or hair pick

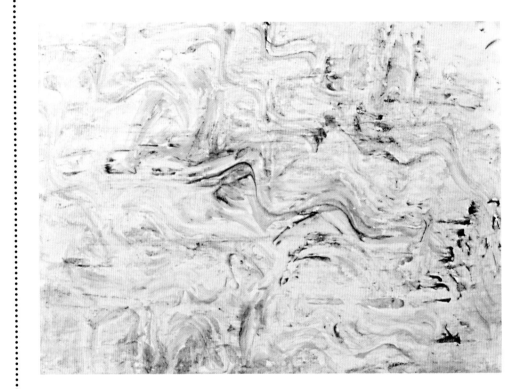

WHAT DO YOU THINK?

This is an experimental and unpredictable way to create beautiful prints that can be used in your cut paper collages or as starting points as background for drawings or paintings. Plan on a lot of time for this as it is a fun process and you will want to keep going!

Fig. 1

Fig. 2

Fig. 3

Fig. 4

Fig. 5

Fig. 6

LET'S GO!

1. Spray the shaving cream onto the tray a little larger than the card stock size you have chosen. (Fig. 1.)

2. With your plastic scraper, smooth the surface of the shaving cream to make it flat. Dispense the craft paint onto the paper plate using as many colors as desired. Add a drop or two of water to each color with a dripping-wet paintbrush. (Fig. 2.)

3. Using the wet paintbrush, drop dots of paint on the shaving cream. Wash your brush between colors, adding dots all over the surface of the shaving cream. (Fig. 3.)

4. Using the fork or hair pick, gently swirl the colors as you like. Place the paper on top of the shaving cream and press gently. (Fig. 4.)

5. Pull off the paper. Some cream will stick to the paper. (Fig. 5.)

6. Using the scraper, shave off the cream to reveal your print! Let it dry. (Fig. 6.)

PAPER NATURE PRINTS

MATERIALS

- reference book of botanicals, seed catalog, or live plants
- pencil
- card stock
- scissors
- masking tape
- two Plexiglas sheets
- water-based block printing ink in 2 colors
- brayer
- paper
- newspaper

WHAT DO YOU THINK?

Do you ever notice the endless shapes in nature? In leaves or plants, in your own backyard or a nearby park, there are endless forms to be found. Many artists use these forms in their work. A famous French artist named Henri Matisse created beautiful plant shapes with cut paper collage. What plants inspire you with their shapes? This lesson allows you to create your own botanical shapes based on real plants.

LET'S GO!

1. Choose some plants to use as models. Draw them with pencil on the card stock and cut them out with scissors. (Figs. 1 and 2.)

2. Use masking tape, form a border on the Plexiglas sheet the same size as the card stock. On a separate Plexiglas sheet, roll out one ink color with the brayer. Roll the ink inside half of the space on the first Plexiglas sheet. (Fig. 3.)

3. Put your cut-out plant shapes on top of the ink. (Fig. 4.)

4. Line up the card stock with the tape and press all over with your hands using firm pressure. Peel off the print. Remove the shapes from the paper if they stuck in the process. (Fig. 5.)

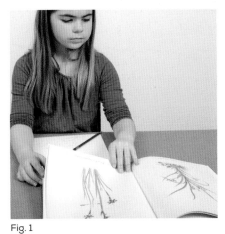

Fig. 1

Fig. 2

Fig. 3

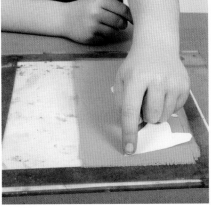

Fig. 4

Fig. 5

5. Add a second ink color to the remaining side of the printing plate as you did with the first. Add the cut-out plant shapes on top of the new ink color. (Fig. 6.)

6. Place the printed card stock on the new ink color and rub as before. Peel off the print and remove any cut shapes that may stick to the ink. (Fig. 7.)

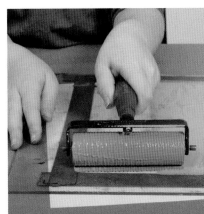

Fig. 6

Fig. 7

STRING TUBE PRINTING

MATERIALS

- ▸ scissors
- ▸ cotton string
- ▸ twine
- ▸ masking tape
- ▸ paper tube
- ▸ brayer
- ▸ printmaking ink or acrylic paint
- ▸ plexiglas sheet
- ▸ paintbrush, if using acrylic paint
- ▸ container of water, if using acrylic paint
- ▸ paper
- ▸ newspaper

WHAT DO YOU THINK?

This lesson teaches you to make a printmaking tool you can use to create textured papers. It can be used in a painting, or even as a first layer of a drawing as it could represent so many things that have texture! You'll decide what kind and how much string you use, what colors the inks will be, and how you will print with it.

Fig. 1

Fig. 2

Fig. 3

Fig. 4

Fig. 5

Fig. 6

LET'S GO!

1. Cut a length of string as long as your arm. (Fig. 1.)

2. Tape one end near the end of the tube. (Fig. 2.)

3. Wrap it around the tube tightly. Tape it securely at the other end. (Fig. 3.)

4. Roll out the ink onto the Plexiglas sheet with the brayer. If you are using acrylic paint, you can simply brush it on with a wet brush. (Fig. 4.)

5. Roll the tube into the ink. (Fig. 5.)

6. Place your paper on top of the newspaper. Press down on the tube and roll it over your papers as desired. Reapply the ink and repeat using as many colors as you like for your design. Before changing colors, simply roll on newspaper until the tube does not print anymore. (Fig. 6.)

UNIT

5

EXPRESS YOURSELF WITH MIXED MEDIA

"I wanted to support things that are helpful to people and maybe bash what I think is dangerous. So I switched from being everybody to being myself."
—JENNY HOLZER

From string and wire to paint, pastels, and papier-mâché: mixed-media art wins over the most hesitant student. Creating art using more than one medium often comes as a relief, as well as a joy, to the maker. These labs include 2D and 3D projects ranging from paintings, collages, and stitching to sculptural projects in wire, weaving, and papier-mâché. There is something exciting and unexpected about gluing a special piece of paper to a painting to create a leaf or stitching a line on paper instead of using a crayon.

Mixed media seems to have no boundaries—and that is a perfect place for self-expression to thrive!

CIRCLE STITCHED MOBILE

MATERIALS

- compass or circular objects to trace
- pencil
- card stock
- scissors
- ruler
- embroidery floss
- needle threader (optional, but handy)
- embroidery needle
- colored pencils
- watercolor or gouache paints
- paintbrush
- container of water

WHAT DO YOU THINK?

Did you know that artists sometimes use stitching with thread to create artwork? Have you ever tried stitching? It can be just like drawing a line with thread instead of a pencil! In this lesson, we will stitch on paper circles and create a sculpture called a *mobile*.

LET'S GO!

1. Using a compass or circular objects to trace, draw one large and three smaller circles on the cardstock with pencil. (Fig. 1.)

2. Cut out the circles. Lightly draw three or four lines through the center to create a guide for your stitches. Repeat the design on the other side. You could also make up your own lines—just keep them simple! (Fig. 2.)

3. Cut a piece of embroidery floss that is as long as your arm from the elbow to wrist. Thread your needle with the floss and tie a knot at the long end. Begin stitching the largest circle by poking the needle up through the paper and pulling the needle and floss all the way through until the knot reaches the paper. (Fig. 3.)

Fig. 1

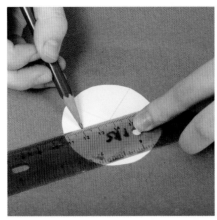

Fig. 2

Fig. 3

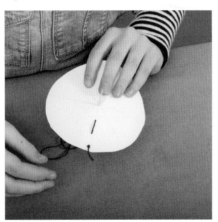
Fig. 4

Fig. 5

all the circles. After stitching, add colored pencil designs or paint as desired.

6. Cut three different lengths of floss. These will be the hanger for your mobile.

7. Thread your needle with one of the lengths you cut in step 6 and make a knot in the end of the long end. On the large circle, stitch each of the three equal lengths of floss from the back to the front on points near the outer edge to create a triangle. The loose ends will be tied together so the circle will hang horizontally, as shown, and be a base for the smaller circles to hang from. (Fig. 5.)

8. Stitch the smaller circles to the large circle at the same three triangle points so they hang below the larger circle. Vary the lengths and tie the knots on each at the top of the large circle. You may attach the smaller circles on end so they hang vertically or through the middle to hang horizontally as our student did!

4. Poke your needle down through the paper to pull the floss all the way through until your first stitch appears! (Fig. 4.)

5. Continue this back-to-front stitching, creating your lines with stitches. When your floss runs out, rethread your needle. Continue stitching on

WIRE WONDERS

MATERIALS

- pencil
- paper
- scrap wood; for younger children use craft foam as the base
- safety glasses
- drill and drill bits—to be used by the adult
- adult to do the drilling
- sandpaper
- wire cutters
- flexible wire; for younger children use extra-long chenille stems
- hot glue gun and glue—to be used by the adult

LET'S GO!

1. Draw a few sketches with pencil on paper of what your sculpture might look like. Using three wires is a good starting point. It can evolve as you work with the wire so stay open to exciting changes! (Fig. 1.)

2. On the wood block, mark with a pencil where you would like the wires to go into the base. Each section of wire will have two ends, so each will need a hole to secure it. Have an

WHAT DO YOU THINK?

We have all drawn lines with all sorts of materials on paper, but in this lesson, we make our line 3-D—off the paper! Many artists use wire to create art that is three-dimensional. It stands up on its own or out from a wall and is called *sculpture*. For this lesson, you will draw with the wire to create your forms. The wood will act as a base to hold it in place. One famous American artist named Alexander Calder created many wire sculptures. See some of his wire sculptures at Calder.org.

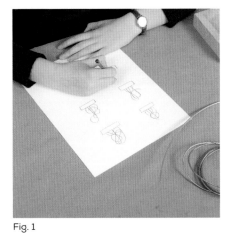

Fig. 1

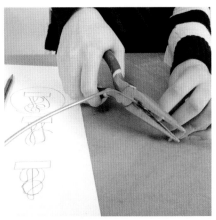

Fig. 3

Fig. 5

Fig. 2

Fig. 4

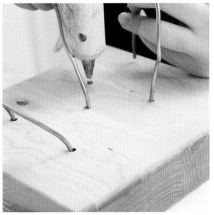

Fig. 6

adult wearing safety glasses drill holes the same size as your wire's gauge into the wooden block at the points you marked.

3. Sand the wood block with the sandpaper to make it smooth. (Fig. 2.)

4. Using the wire cutters, cut the first length of wire as long as you think it should be. Consider extra length for curves and loops! (Fig. 3.)

5. Put one end of a length of wire into a hole in the base. Bend the remaining wire as desired to form the first lines of your sculpture. The other end should end up in a hole in your wooden base. (Fig. 4.)

6. Continue as in steps 4 and 5 to complete your sculpture. Adjust the wires as needed to get the sculpture to look the way you want. (Fig. 5.)

7. Have an adult add a drop of hot glue to each hole to secure the wires in place. (Fig. 6.)

8. Options for younger children: Use a Styrofoam base and extra long chenille stems for a similar effect.

WOVEN EYE

MATERIALS

- large piece of cardboard
- pencil
- an adult to cut the cardboard
- scissors
- scrap of wood
- hammer
- nail
- string
- oil pastels
- watercolor paints
- paintbrush
- container of water
- yarn in various weights and colors
- masking tape

WHAT DO YOU THINK?

Weaving is an art form that has been around for thousands of years all over the world. This weaving lesson asks you to create an eye with mixed media—oil pastels, paint, and then string and yarn to form the iris and pupil of the eye. The eye has been a focus in artwork, such as in René Magritte's *The False Mirror*, and a prominent image in Egyptian and modern art. Think about what shape your eye will be and the colors you will choose to express your idea of a woven eye!

Fig. 1

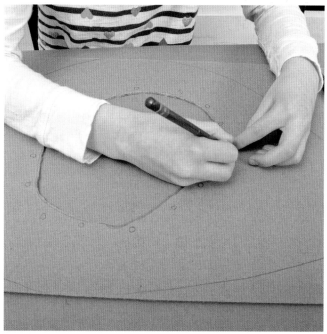

Fig. 2

Fig. 3

LET'S GO!

1. Using the pencil, draw the shape of an eye on the cardboard. Draw the iris and eyelids and eyelashes as desired. The pupil will be cut out for the weaving. (Fig. 1.)

2. Have an adult cut out the pupil. (Fig. 2.)

3. Mark an odd number of dots with pencil all around the iris. Our student drew fifteen. This will be where you string your loom.

4. Place the wood underneath the drawing, where you just marked the dots, to protect the work surface. Use the hammer and nail to create holes where the dots are. (Fig. 3.) Wiggle the nail in the hole to make it big enough for your string to pass through. (Fig. 4.)

(continued)

Fig. 4

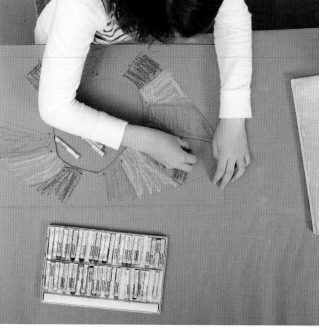

Fig. 5

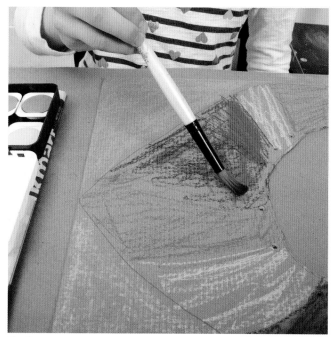

Fig. 6

5. Add color to the iris with oil pastels. Add details to the background such as words, color, eyelashes, or designs! (Fig. 5.)

6. Add watercolor paint over the oil pastels to make your colors pop! Let it dry. (Fig. 6.)

7. Cut a piece of string about 2 yards (1.8 m) long. Use the string to create the loom by threading it through a hole from the back and then through the hole across from it as shown. Continue by threading the string across the pupil and all the way around the pupil ending on the back. Tape the end down with masking tape. (Fig. 7.)

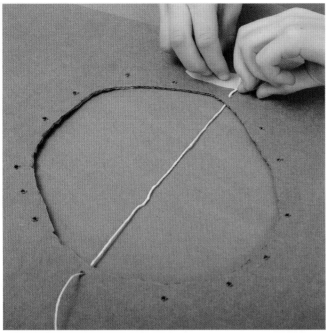

Fig. 7

Fig. 8

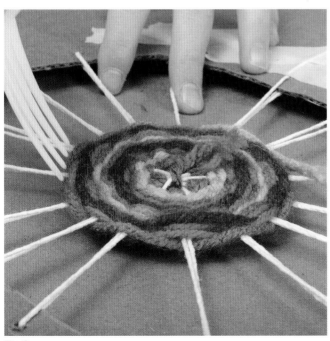

Fig. 9

8. Cut a piece of yarn about 2 yards (1.8 m) long and wind it up in a small ball to make it easy to pass through your string loom. Begin by finding the center of your pupil where all the strings cross, and tie the end of the yarn to the center of the strings with the knot on the backside. (Fig. 8.)

9. Begin weaving. Bring the ball of yarn to the front of the eye and go over the first string. Then bring the yarn under the next string, continuing over and under until you run out of yarn. Don't pull the yarn too tight and make sure it is not too loose. Tie a new length of yarn onto the end of the first piece and continue weaving the pupil of the eye as far as you wish! Use a fork to gently push the weaving together as shown. Tie the end in a knot on the back. (Fig. 9.)

MIXED-MEDIA COLLAGE

MATERIALS

- scissors
- discarded magazines
- paper
- glue stick
- oil pastels in various colors
- watercolor paints in various colors
- watercolor paintbrush
- container of water
- newspaper

 **WHAT DO YOU THINK?**

Drawing with paper, paint, and pastels can be a fun mixture of media. If you have some old magazines or recycled paper bins, you can start collecting art materials right away! For this lesson, you will use paper for the subject matter and oil pastel and paint for the setting.

Fig. 1

Fig. 2

Fig. 3

Fig. 4

Fig. 5

Fig. 6

LET'S GO!

1. Decide what your subject will be and where it will live.

2. Cut or tear pages of color and textured photographs from magazines. Find all the colors and textures you will need for your subject. (Fig. 1.)

3. Sort the paper scraps into piles by color. (Fig. 2.)

4. Cut and layout the collage pieces on the paper to form the subject. (Fig. 3.)

5. Glue the collage pieces to your paper. Press firmly. (Fig. 4.)

6. Using oil pastels, draw the setting for the subject. (Fig. 5.)

7. Finish the setting by painting it with watercolors. Let it dry. (Fig. 6.)

ART TROPHIES

MATERIALS

▸ cardboard pieces and other recycled materials
▸ masking tape
▸ small quart-size (1.1 L) container
▸ white all-purpose flour
▸ water
▸ newspaper
▸ acrylic paints including metallic colors
▸ sequins, chenille stems, and shiny papers for added pizzazz! (optional)

LET'S GO!

1. Gather some cardboard recyclables. (Fig. 1.)

2. Try putting different pieces together to create an idea. This is sketching directly with materials. (Fig. 2.)

3. Begin assembling the armature, or skeleton, of your trophy. Use masking tape to secure the pieces together firmly. (Fig. 3.)

4. When the armature is complete, you can begin to papier-mâché your trophy. In a small container, mix up three parts water with one part flour until smooth. Rip some newspaper into strips. (Fig. 4.)

5. Dip a strip of newspaper into the flour and water mixture and smooth off the excess over the container.

WHAT DO YOU THINK?

When you create art that you love and are proud of, the art itself is a trophy. However, it is also a lot of fun to show off a trophy for your hard work! This lesson helps you design and create the trophy of your dreams that is a sculptural work of art as well!

Fig. 1

Fig. 2

Fig. 3

Fig. 4

Fig. 5

6. Starting at the bottom, place the strip on the trophy and smooth it over the armature. Continue using the papier-mâché technique from the bottom up until the armature is covered completely. Let it dry and cover it with a second layer for strength. Let it dry. (Fig. 5.)

7. Once dry, add any details you'd like, first with masking tape then covered with papier-mâché. Let it dry. (Fig. 6.)

8. Paint as desired and add any embellishments you like. Metallic paint is great! (Fig. 7.)

Fig. 6

Fig. 7

PLASTER RELIEF

MATERIALS

- small panel of wood
- paper
- pencil
- scissors
- paper tubes
- joint compound
- plastic knives
- twine
- watercolor paints in various colors
- watercolor paintbrush
- container of water

WHAT DO YOU THINK?

Many artists carve, assemble, or mold materials on a flat surface to create a sculpture to hang on a wall. This is called *relief sculpture*. In this lesson, you will work three dimensionally and build up the surface as far as you wish ending with a sculpture to hang on a wall. Our student chose a face to sculpt, but you can try any subject—from landscape to abstract or still life!

LET'S GO!

1. Trace around your wood base with pencil on paper. Sketch your subject inside that space for an exact size. (Fig. 1.) Cut up some of your paper tubes to create raised elements in your drawing.

2. Spread the joint compound with a plastic knife onto the wood. As you spread it, you can add texture with the knife or make it smooth. The compound should be about ¼ inch (6 mm) thick on the base. Our compound is pink when wet but dries to a white color. This helps us know when to stop working with it. Others compounds work as well. (Fig. 2.)

3. Draw your design into the wet compound with a pencil.

Fig. 1

Fig. 2

Fig. 3

Fig. 4

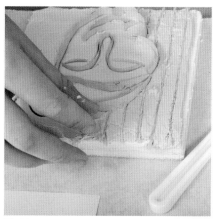
Fig. 5

4. Add the paper tube pieces to the wet compound. Press them down firmly. (Figs. 3 and 4.)

5. Add a background with pieces of twine or additional cut-up paper tubes. Other items such as beads, tissue paper, or yarn also work in the compound. (Fig. 5.) Let it dry overnight.

6. Once dry, you are ready to paint. Using watercolor paints and a damp but not overly wet paintbrush, paint the subject and the tubes. (Fig. 6.)

7. Finish by painting the background. Let it dry and it will be ready to hang. (Fig. 7.)

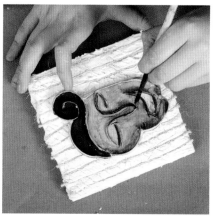
Fig. 6

Fig. 7

PLASTIC ASSEMBLAGE

MATERIALS

▸ plastic marker covers from used markers or other colorful plastic items, such as bottlecaps, paperclips, buttons, bread tags, small lids
▸ wood panel for base
▸ clear glue

LET'S GO!

1. Sort your plastic objects by color. (Fig. 1.)

2. Begin arranging them on the wood panel—try different combinations to decide what you like best. (Fig. 2.)

WHAT DO YOU THINK?

This lesson was directly inspired by artists Lisa Solomon and Christine Buckton Tillman's "Chroma" installation of recycled plastic objects. In the Gallery of Artists (page 138) you will find more information about this. We use marker caps we have saved for a while and we asked some of our friends to save them, too! An *assemblage* is a sculpture that can hang from the wall or other surface. This project is all about color and how you want to express it in 3-D.

Fig. 1

Fig. 2

Fig. 3

Fig. 4

Fig. 5

3. Apply plenty of glue to the wood base panel and begin gluing the pieces onto the base. (Figs. 3 and 4.)

4. Stack some objects in layers, if desired, after the first layer is dry. Press them into the glue and let dry. (Fig. 5.)

SAY IT WITH STITCHES

MATERIALS

- pencil
- paper
- foam core panel
- plain white T-shirt
- fabric paint or acrylic paint and textile medium
- soft paintbrush
- embroidery hoop
- scissors
- embroidery floss
- embroidery needle

WHAT DO YOU THINK?

Words are often used in art, including paintings, prints, textiles, and sculpture. In this lesson, you can choose a word or short phrase to create a shirt that expresses something you want to tell the world in your very own writing!

LET'S GO!

1. Draw a few ideas of a word or words you want to express with pencil on paper. Take time creating your letters' shapes. (Fig. 1.)

2. Slide the foam core inside the T-shirt to create a flat surface to work on and to protect the paint from leaking through to the back of the shirt. Lightly sketch the letters onto the shirt with the pencil. (Fig. 2.)

3. Using fabric paint, or acrylic paint with textile medium, paint your letters with a soft paintbrush. (Fig. 3.) Let it dry.

4. Place one side of the embroidery hoop over the words and the other part inside the shirt to stretch it flat. (Fig. 4.) Decide if you will stitch around the edge of each letter or around the words, as we did.

Fig. 1

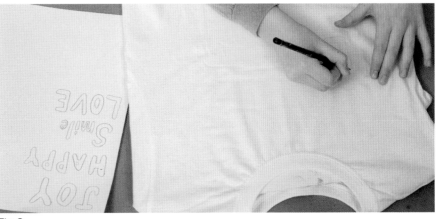
Fig. 2

Fig. 3

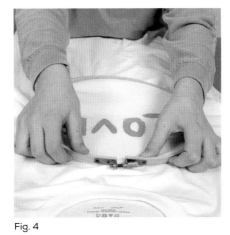
Fig. 4

Fig. 5

Fig. 6

5. Cut a piece of embroidery floss the length of your arm. Thread the needle with the floss and tie a knot at the long end. Beginning on the inside of the shirt, push the needle up through the shirt and then back down through the fabric to create a stitch. Keep the stitches small so they don't become too loose. Don't pull the stitches too tightly. Rethread the needle when you run out of thread and remember to tie a knot at the end of your thread! (Fig. 5.)

6. Continue around the letters or word until complete! (Fig. 6.)

ALL THAT GLITTERS

MATERIALS

- pencil
- card stock
- oil pastels in various colors
- watercolor paints in various colors
- paintbrushes
- container of water
- clear glue
- plastic lid
- newspaper
- glitter

WHAT DO YOU THINK?

What would you like to make glittery and sparkly that in real life isn't? What special thing will you choose? In this mixed-media lesson, we will add a lot of sparkle to our paintings to make our subject matter shine brightly.

LET'S GO!

1. With a pencil, draw out your idea on card stock. (Fig. 1.)

2. Add color over your pencil lines with the oil pastels. Leave large areas open for watercolor paints. (Fig. 2.)

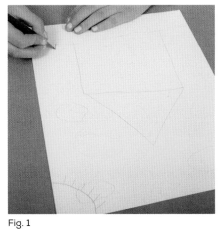

Fig. 1

Fig. 2

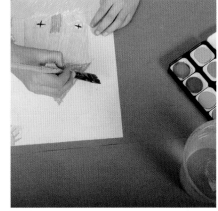

Fig. 3

Fig. 4

Fig. 5

3. Using the watercolors, paint in the areas you left open or want to add more color to. (Fig. 3.)

4. Dispense some clear glue onto the plastic lid. Put the sheet of newspaper under your painting. (Fig. 4.)

5. Using a clean paintbrush, apply glue to the areas where you want the glitter to be. (Fig. 5.)

6. Sprinkle the glitter on the glued areas. Pick up your painting, keeping it flat, and gently tap it to spread the glitter. (Fig. 6.)

7. When finished with the glitter, tap the paper, as shown, on the newspaper to remove any excess. (Fig. 7.)

Fig. 6

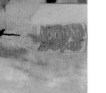

Fig. 7

FEELINGS POTS

MATERIALS

▸ colorful oven-bake clay, such as Sculpey brand
▸ aluminum foil
▸ oven
▸ adult to help with baking

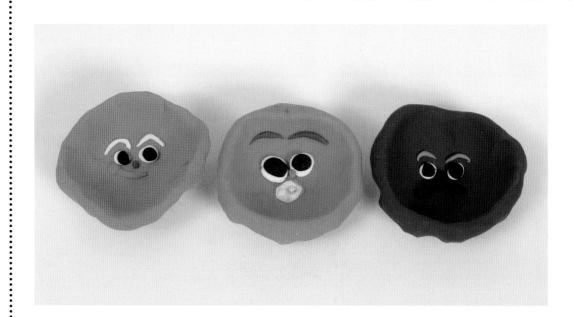

 WHAT DO YOU THINK?

Showing our feelings through art is a natural way to express ourselves. Many artists use their feelings and opinions to guide their work. In this lesson, we will create small, colorful pinch pots to show a range of emotions.

LET'S GO!

1. Choose three or four emotions to use in this project. Select clay colors that represent your emotions the best. Roll each color into a small ball that will fit comfortably in the palm of your hand. (Fig. 1.)

Fig. 1

Fig. 2

Fig. 3

Fig. 4

2. Using your thumb and forefinger, pinch a small opening in one ball and start forming the side walls of the pot with a gentle pinching motion around the hole. The walls should be the same thickness as the bottom of the pot. (Fig. 2.)

3. Using some of the other clay colors, form features such as eyes, eyebrows, a nose, and mouth as well as ears or other details you choose. Remember, these details should express the emotion you chose. If you are unsure of what it should look like, look in a mirror and make a face to represent the emotion. What details do you see? Press the details firmly onto the pot with your finger, a toothpick, or wooden skewer. (Fig. 3.)

4. The features can appear on the outside of the pot or on the bottom of the inside—you choose! (Fig. 4.)

5. Have an adult bake the clay pots according the manufacturer's instructions on the package.

SCRAP WOOD SCULPTURE

MATERIALS

- small scraps of wood
- white glue
- acrylic paint (optional)
- paintbrushes
- container of water
- newspaper

WHAT DO YOU THINK?

Sometimes, scraps from other people's work can be considered new materials for you to create something. We have collected small wood scraps for creating sculptures for a long time. Check your local lumberyard as they often will give them away. What would you build with pieces of wood? This project creates tabletop-size sculptures inspired by larger pieces by famous artist Louise Nevelson and our friend Adam Pearson, whose work is in the Gallery of Artists (page 138).

Fig. 1

Fig. 2

Fig. 3

Fig. 4

LET'S GO!

1. Select a piece of wood from your scraps to be the base. Look over the other scraps and sort out the ones you like best. Arrange them in as many different ways as possible to choose what formations you like best. (Fig. 1.)

2. Glue the bottom pieces of your formation to the base. (Fig. 2.)

3. Work your way up using plenty of glue. If you want to speed up drying time, use a hair dryer. Otherwise, just let the glue dry before going too high! (Fig. 3.)

4. When the sculpture is dry, you may paint it if you like. Use the acrylic paint for this and wash out your brush between colors. (Fig. 4.)

BALLOON BEAD SCULPTURE

MATERIALS

- newspaper
- bowl
- all-purpose flour
- water
- balloons, different shapes are fun to use
- balloon-like packing pillows
- wax paper
- masking tape (optional)
- paper egg carton (optional)
- one 4-foot (1.2 m) piece of 1-inch (2.5 cm) -diameter dowel
- acrylic paint in various colors
- paintbrushes
- container of water
- recycled quart-size (about 1 l) plastic container with lid, such as a yogurt container
- scissors
- an adult to mix the plaster
- plaster
- Mod Podge
- paper plate
- paper tubes, for spacer beads (optional)

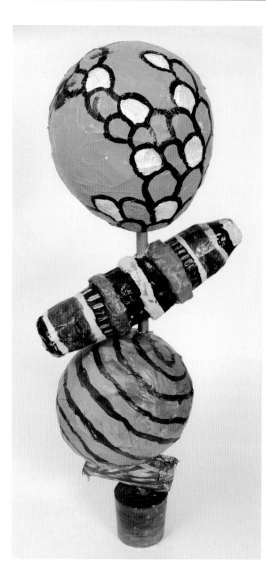

Fig. 1

Fig. 2

WHAT DO YOU THINK?

Papier-mâché is a great, inexpensive medium for making large, lightweight sculptures. It takes time to build up the layers, but that is part of the fun. This sculpture is based on jewelry beads that are stacked on a dowel instead of a necklace chain. An adult will be needed to help mix the plaster for the base. You can design your beads in the style of your choice—there is no limit to what you can do with this sculpture! What message could your beads send? What do you want to show the world?

LET'S GO!

1. Tear up strips of newspaper. In your bowl, mix together three parts water with one part flour. Blow up the balloons you will use. If you use packing pillows, they are ready to go. Start by placing the first balloon in a container to hold it. Have a sheet of waxed paper handy to place the balloon on to dry. (Fig. 1.)

2. Dip a strip of newspaper in the flour and water mixture and remove the excess as shown. (Fig. 2.)

(continued)

Fig. 3

Fig. 4

3. Smooth the wet newspaper over the balloon. Continue wetting and placing the strips until the balloon is covered. Let it dry on the wax paper and then add a second layer of strips. Cover all the balloons in this fashion. If you like, add bumps and ridges between the first dried layer and the second layer with masking tape and small wads of newspaper or paper egg carton pieces. Simply tape them on with masking tape and smooth the second layer over the add-ons. (Fig. 3.)

4. When all the balloons have had two layers of papier-mâché applied and are dry, paint them in colors you like. (Fig. 4.) Let dry on waxed paper.

5. Have an adult cut a hole in the center of the lid of the quart (about 1 l) container that is the same size as the dowel. Folding it in half makes easy work of this! Have the adult mix up the plaster in the container according to the package directions. Put the lid on the container and place the dowel into the plaster-filled container almost to the bottom. Let the plaster dry for 24 hours. Have an adult cut off the plastic container when dry.

Fig. 5

6. Add any painted details to any of the papier-mâché beads. Paint the base and dowel. Let everything dry. Seal each papier-mâché bead and the base with a coat of Mod Podge. (Fig. 5.)

7. Decide where the holes will be cut by holding the bead up to the dowel and marking it with a pencil. Cut out the hole with scissors—ask an adult to poke it through if you need help.

8. Stack the beads on the dowel. The last bead will only need one hole. If you like, decorate cardboard tubes with paint and use them between beads as spacers. (Fig. 6.)

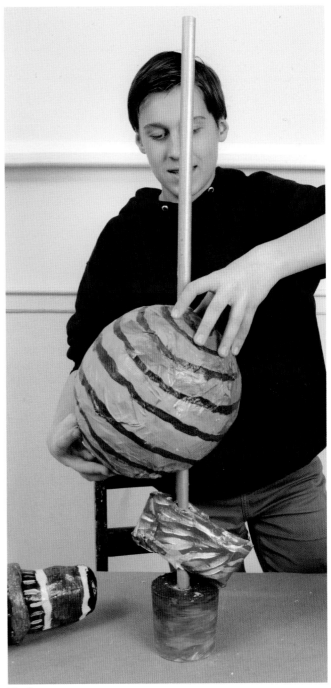

Fig. 6

EXPRESS YOURSELF WITH PAPER

"One eye sees, the other feels."
–PAUL KLEE

Paper is essential in the art room as either a base or a springboard for creating. This chapter looks to paper as an inspiration as much as a medium. Using everyday papers, such as newspaper, cardboard, safety envelopes, and discarded books, magazines, and sheet music, a world of cut-paper collage can open up! By adding a few other art supplies, artwork based in paper can be versatile as well as affordable.

This chapter tears, cuts, pastes, and weaves your ideas into new experiences each time you work through a lesson. Paper can inspire you to create and to be fearless in the process because it isn't an overly precious material. Paper is familiar and yet can be transformed into artwork unique to your vision.

LAB 45

COLORFUL BEASTS

MATERIALS

▸ reference images of endangered animals
▸ pencil
▸ drawing paper
▸ eraser
▸ tissue paper in various colors
▸ scissors
▸ glue stick

 WHAT DO YOU THINK?

Do you know there are many endangered, or vulnerable, animals? Take a few minutes and check out the list online. Choose an animal that is important to you, and we will make a collage painting of it in this lesson!

There was a group of artists in Europe during the early 1900s called the Blue Rider that created artwork about nature in bright and bold colors. This was during a time when people were more interested in machines and factories than nature. This group wanted to remind people how important and beautiful the natural world was and made art that people noticed through the use of color. We will do the same in this lesson!

Fig. 1

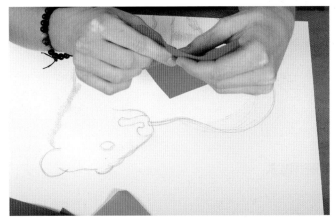
Fig. 2

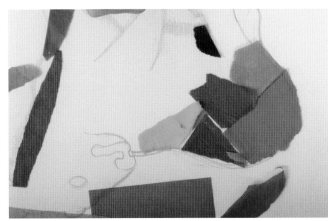
Fig. 3

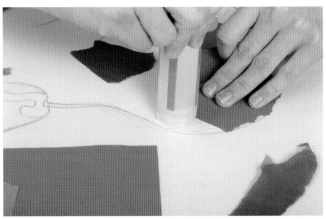
Fig. 4

LET'S GO!

1. With a pencil, lightly draw the animal's outline, or contour, on your paper. Add minimal details. (Fig. 1.)

2. Choose the tissue paper colors that you want to express your animal. Our student chose multiple colors to represent a white polar bear.

3. Begin tearing paper to fit your animal's shape. Work in small sections. (Fig. 2.)

4. Overlap pieces for a different look. (Fig. 3.)

5. Use scissors to cut small pieces or details or repeated shapes.

6. Apply glue to the drawing paper in small sections and press the tissue into place. (Fig. 4.)

7. Add a background with additional tissue paper, if you like!

I BUILT THIS CITY

MATERIALS

▸ newspaper
▸ scissors
▸ card stock
▸ watercolors
▸ watercolor paintbrush
▸ container of water
▸ glue stick
▸ fine-point permanent marker
▸ scrap paper for gluing

WHAT DO YOU THINK?

If you could build a city, what would it look like? What would be going on in, around, and on top of the buildings? Who might live there?

LET'S GO!

1. Open a newspaper and take a look at the columns of text. Do you notice how they look like buildings of different sizes and shapes? (Fig. 1.)

2. Cut out some building shapes that you see in the columns of text. Cut out more than you think you will need. Think about the rooftop shapes and the building sizes. (Fig. 2.)

Fig. 1

Fig. 2

Fig. 3

Fig. 4

Fig. 5

Fig. 6

3. Lay the buildings out on the card stock, which will become the background of your city. Do they touch each other or overlap? (Fig. 3.)

4. Put the buildings aside and get ready to paint the background of your city. Think about what time of day it is and what season it is in your city.

5. With watercolors, paint the entire paper from the top, or the sky, to the bottom. Wash your brush between colors. Let your background dry. (Fig. 4.)

6. Using the glue stick, apply glue to the back of the buildings and press them firmly to the background. Continue until all the buildings are in place. (Fig. 5.)

7. If you like, use your fine-point marker to add details to the buildings, windows for example. You may also add watercolor to them or just keep them black and white! (Fig. 6.)

LAB 47

TINY SKETCHBOOK IDEAS

MATERIALS

- index cards
- pens
- colored pencils
- hammer
- nail
- scissors
- embroidery floss or waxed linen thread
- tiny beads (optional)

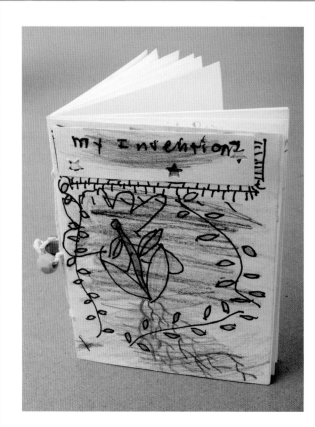

WHAT DO YOU THINK?

Do you like to think up inventions? Have you ever had some great ideas and wanted to remember them later? This lesson shows you how to make a little book to keep all of your big ideas together. It's tiny so it will be easy to keep in a pocket, ready to record your ideas!

Fig. 1

Fig. 2

Fig. 3

Fig. 4

Fig. 5

Fig. 6

LET'S GO!

1. Fold six or seven index cards in half as shown. Crease the folds well. (Fig. 1.)

2. Place them inside each other to form the book. (Fig. 2.)

3. The first card will be your cover. Choose a title for your sketchbook and write it on the front cover with pen or colored pencil. You can also add a drawing, if you like! (Fig. 3.)

4. Place your book, with the cover on the bottom, on top of your scrap wood. Open the book to the center page. Using the nail and hammer, make two holes on the fold—the first hole 1 inch (2.5 cm) from the top and the second hole 1 inch (2.5 cm) from the bottom. Hammer the nail through all the pages. (Fig. 4.)

5. Cut a piece of floss or thread that is twice as long as your book's fold. From the inside center page, thread one end through the top hole and one end through the bottom hole. (Fig. 5.)

6. Flip the book over and tie a knot with the two ends on the outside fold (called the book's spine) to hold the book together. Add beads onto the thread, if you like! (Fig. 6.)

MAKE A FACE

MATERIALS

- ► 3 small containers, to mix the paint
- ► gesso
- ► acrylic paint in 3 colors
- ► craft sticks or plastic spoons, to mix the paint
- ► cardboard pieces in various sizes
- ► 3 bristle brushes, one for each paint color
- ► paper plate
- ► clear glue
- ► oil pastels in various colors
- ► newspaper

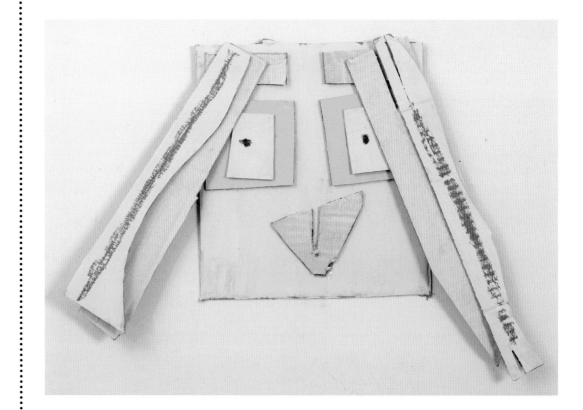

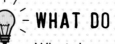 WHAT DO YOU THINK?

What does your face look like when you are happy, or sad, or silly? Where are your eyebrows when you are surprised? What colors do you think express anger? Choose a feeling and let's make a face!

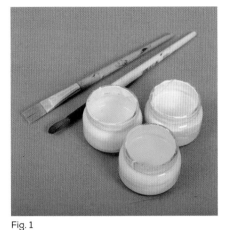

Fig. 1

Fig. 2

Fig. 3

Fig. 4

Fig. 5

Fig. 6

LET'S GO!

1. In your small containers—use one for each paint color—combine equal amounts of gesso and acrylic paint. Stir thoroughly. (Fig. 1.)

2. Choose the pieces of cardboard that will represent your face, including all the details you want to show. Think eyebrows, hair, cheeks, nose, ears, lips, or other details to express your emotion. (Fig. 2.)

3. Arrange the cardboard pieces to create your face and decide which color each piece will be. Put the pieces into three piles sorted by color. (Fig. 3.)

4. Paint each pile in its designated color and let dry on the paper plate. Wash your brushes in the sink. (Fig. 4.)

5. Reassemble your face and glue the back of each detail to the cardboard face. Press hard! (Fig. 5.)

6. Let dry overnight. The next day, add more details with oil pastels, if you like. (Fig. 6.)

TEAR ME A TULIP

MATERIALS

▸ colorful paper
▸ tissue paper
▸ glue stick
▸ ribbon (optional)

WHAT DO YOU THINK?

Did you ever pick flowers to give someone? Do you ever find a dandelion or daisy growing wild near where you live? Perhaps you have a garden where tulips and other flowers grow but can't be picked. Think of your favorite flowers and their shapes. Let's make a paper bouquet.

LET'S GO!

1. Choose a piece of colorful paper for the background.

2. Choose three or more colors of tissue paper and colored paper for your flowers. Check their colors against the background color you chose. You can always change your mind if you don't like how it looks.

3. Using your fingers, slowly tear the flower shapes from the paper. Make layers of petals for each flower and keep them in piles. (Fig. 1.)

4. Layout the flowers on the background, arranging them as you wish. Move them around until you find an arrangement you like. Now tear the stems and leaves in the same manner. (Fig. 2.)

Fig. 1

Fig. 2

Fig. 3

Fig. 4

Fig. 5

5. Using the glue stick, glue the blossoms to the background, pressing firmly with your fingertips. (Fig. 3.)

6. Decide if the flowers will be a bouquet or an arrangement in a vase. (Fig. 4.)

7. If you choose a vase, tear one out of the colorful paper.

8. Glue the stems, leaves, and vase to the background, adding a ribbon if desired. (Fig. 5.)

A BIRD IN THE HAND

MATERIALS

▸ colored paper in various colors
▸ a friend
▸ pencil
▸ scissors
▸ glue stick
▸ scrap paper for applying the glue

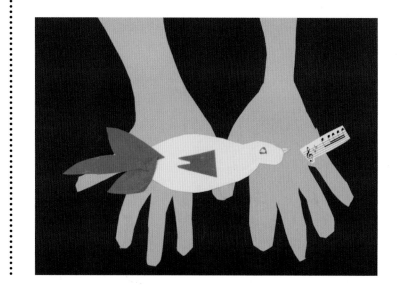

WHAT DO YOU THINK?

Proverbs are brief, popular sayings that illustrate a moral lesson. For this lesson, I chose, "A bird in the hand is worth two in the bush." What does this mean to you? What do you have that you are thankful for? It can be anything you are glad you have! My student chose a baby chick, as she loves the eggs they provide her family—an actual bird in the hand!

LET'S GO!

1. Choose two large pieces of paper with colors that you like together; one will be the background and the other for your hands.

2. Have a friend trace your hands and arm up to your wrist, or a little further, with a pencil on one piece of paper you selected. You can also try to do this yourself! (Fig. 1.)

3. Cut out the hand drawings. (Fig. 2.)

4. What did you decide you were thankful for? Choose a smaller piece of paper and draw the item on it, then cut it out! (Fig. 3.)

Fig. 1

Fig. 2

Fig. 3

Fig. 4

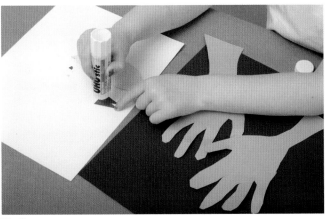

Fig. 5

5. Add details by cutting them out of other pieces of colored paper.

6. Arrange your cut-out hands on the background paper. Using the glue stick, glue the hands onto the paper. (Fig. 4.)

7. Glue your "thankful for" piece into your cut-out hands. (Fig. 5.)

8. Add more details with more cut paper!

TWO-IN-ONE WEAVING

LAB 51

MATERIALS

▸ pencil
▸ two pieces of watercolor paper cut to the same size
▸ colored pencils
▸ watercolor paints
▸ soft watercolor paintbrush
▸ container of water
▸ ruler
▸ scissors
▸ glue stick
▸ mat board

WHAT DO YOU THINK?

Do you ever have a couple of good ideas at the same time and can't decide which one to use? In this lesson, you will combine them into one through weaving. There are many different ways to choose subject matter for this lesson. It can be something in nature, a drawing of a friend or pet, a favorite food—anything you like. Our student combined a cherry blossom drawing with the fruit itself! First, think and sketch some ideas, and stretch your imagination to find unexpected combinations.

LET'S GO!

1. Begin sketching with pencil, if desired, and then add colored pencil to your drawing. (Fig. 1.)

2. Add watercolor paints as you like. (Fig. 2.)

3. With a ruler and your pencil, draw vertical lines on the back of the first drawing; draw horizontal lines on the back of the second drawing. These lines can be as far apart as 1 inch (2.5 cm) or closer as shown. (Fig. 3.)

4. Cut the drawings on the lines and lay the pieces out in order as you go. (Fig. 4.)

5. Using the glue stick, glue the tops of the vertically cut drawing to the mat board as shown and press firmly. Take the first strip of the horizontally cut paper and weave it **over** the first glued strip and **under** the second glued strip repeating all the way across the vertical strips. (Fig. 5.)

Fig. 1

Fig. 2

Fig. 3

Fig. 4

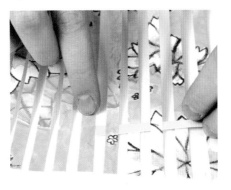

Fig. 5

6. For the second row, start with the second horizontal strip going **under** and then **over** as shown. The third row will go begin **over then under**, as the first row did, and the fourth will **begin under**. Continue in this fashion throughout. (Fig. 6.)

7. When you are finished, add glue stick to the mat board and stick the weaving down to secure it. Place a heavy book on it until it dries. (Fig. 7.)

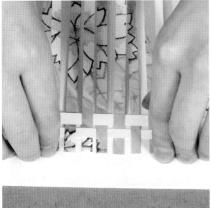

Fig. 6

Fig. 7

A NEW ME COLLAGE

MATERIALS

▸ photocopy of a picture of your head
▸ discarded magazines
▸ scissors
▸ paper
▸ glue stick

WHAT DO YOU THINK?

Paper collage is wonderful medium to express some humor and get a little silly with your art. The materials are simple and can be created on a small space! For this lesson, you can be as animated as you want—perhaps even taking three or four different photos of yourself with different emotions. You can choose your mood or make a collage of multiple "yous."

Fig. 1

Fig. 2

Fig. 3

Fig. 4

LET'S GO!

1. From the photocopy of your face, cut out your head and neck. Begin looking through the magazines for a suitable torso for your head to go with—animals, people, even plants—whatever you choose will work! (Fig. 1.)

2. Choose a few different parts to put together so you will have choices as you go. Do not glue them down yet as you are still arranging and deciding. Look for backgrounds and other surroundings for your composition (Fig. 2.)

3. When you have made all your final choices, glue the pieces in place. Begin with the pieces that are in the background and work your way forward to the pieces closest to you. Use a piece of paper under your magazine pieces for applying the glue to keep the final artwork free from extra glue. (Fig. 3.)

4. Press all edges firmly so they stick to the paper. (Fig. 4.)

GALLERY OF ARTISTS

RACHEL BLUMBERG

The work that I make, the work that I perform, the work that I think about, it all comes from a similar place. There are stories that we all have; there are stories that get woven into the fabric of our every day, into our history, into the well-worn paths we create during our life, that are building blocks of culture and life force.

When I paint, or animate, or drum, or teach, or think about how to combine these things, or collaborate with others, I tap into these stories, and draw inspiration from them in an improvised approach to creating something new. I think that art making, self-expression if you will, is as essential to living as eating and drinking; it is an opportunity for you to go into a place where can create worlds and feelings and fodder for thinking to share with others, or it can be just for yourself. It can be fun; it can be painful; it can be invigorating; it can be frustrating; it can be euphoric!

RACHEL BLUMBERG likes to wear and juggle many hats. She is a teaching artist, a filmmaker specializing in stop-motion animation, a musician/composer specializing in drumming/percussion, and a visual artist. Some people call this multidisciplinary.
www.rachelblumberg.com

JEN CORACE

Drawing and painting have always been important practices in my life. The ability to see, look, and interpret words and ideas into pictures is a problem my brain enjoys solving. I enjoy watching people, looking at objects, seeing how light interacts with spaces, getting lost staring at images on the internet and in art galleries. All of the looking and seeing is important research (whether passive or active) that informs the work I do. Not only does it feed the imagery that will be a part of the composition, it enables me to be a better communicator.

One of the most important aspects of being an illustrator is translating ideas and experiences into a more universal expression. As artists, we are responsible to our audience, no matter how small or large they may be, to step away from our bubble and find a visual common ground that speaks to them. The more I know about the world around me, the more I can connect with the people around me. My experience with art and creating the career that I have has made me more open, more flexible, and more empathetic to the world around me. I am endlessly thankful for that.

JEN CORACE was born and raised in southern New Jersey and was happiest being left alone to draw in her room. Her mom, always her champion, recognized this early on and kept her eyes looking and her drawing hand moving. She has a BFA from RISD in illustration.

www.jencorace.com

ADAM PEARSON

As a kid, I had much fun building things, using tools, scrounging for materials, and just making stuff. When I was old enough, I went to work for my father doing construction. I have always enjoyed landscaping and moving rocks and dirt around. For me, sculpture gives the opportunity to explore the best parts of these different experiences I had growing up and lets me use any of the possible mediums I am drawn to.

Balancing rocks and working with found materials was a way for me to combine landscape design and construction so I could present the end product as sculpture, finding beauty in the decayed and discarded. My favorite material to work with is steel, or really just about any metal, both found and fabricated, but I also enjoy using clay, wood, and stone.

ADAM PEARSON is a sculptor and craftsman. He works in the art department of the University of New Hampshire where he received his BFA.

www.pearsonsculpture.com

MEGHAN SAMSON

How Art Saved Me

I have always been an artist, and cannot remember a time when I did not make things with my hands. I drew things from my life when I was really young. They were a manifestation of my experiences and feelings–a visual diary. I drew pictures of my family in the kitchen or in the woodshop in our barn and of trees and fields at my house. Sketchbooks documented my life. I think art saved me because it was always there for me, like a friend or a part of me that made me feel whole. I never felt lonely if I could make pictures. In high school, I found clay and fell in love with the medium right away. I could make drawings on clay and eventually I could make my drawings into clay forms. They became more physical characters in my story line. They were abstract and imagined, but they represented parts of me and the people I loved. Seen as a whole, my artworks form an intricate, connected web, performing the experiences of family, love, attachment, and self-portrait.

MEGHAN SAMSON has a BFA in clay and sculpture from the University of New Hampshire and received her MFA from Boston University.

www.meghan-samson.com

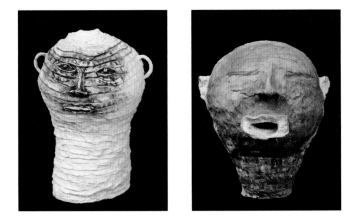

LISA SOLOMON

Making art is a very special endeavor for me. I make it because I love it (even when I'm frustrated by it). It makes me think, it makes me feel, it makes me understand. Art opens my eyes and my heart and my brain to new ideas and to other people's perspectives. When I am having a hard or challenging moment (or day) I just have to think about making something and I start to feel better. I get excited. Sometimes, I get very quiet—which can also be great. Opening myself up to creativity and possibilities is kind of magical. When I am in the studio, I can let go and simply try to express myself. I know that even if something doesn't come out the way I wanted or expected, it is okay. In fact, it might even be better. If I don't like something, that is okay too. It isn't about right or wrong, it's about doing. What else offers that freedom? In our current lives, with so many distractions and obligations (school, phones, jobs, YouTube), art forces me to slow down and it gives me space to

make up my own mind. And when I look at art, I feel connected. Sometimes, it's like a puzzle where I try to figure out what that artist was thinking or trying to convey. I find that so valuable and hope you do, too.

Lisa Solomon and Christine Buckton Tillman, from Baltimore, Maryland, met back in 2004 via the photo-sharing website Flickr. Because of their shared affinity for drawing, the handmade, wall-based installations, and color they connected immediately. They eventually were able to collaborate and work on the installation "Chroma" in 2015, which you see in these images. They have been fortunate enough to create three different versions of "Chroma" from coast to coast— exhibiting it at Gallery CA in Baltimore, Maryland, Rare Device in San Francisco, California, and finally placing it permanently in a building at the Wharf in Washington, DC.

LISA SOLOMON is a mixed-media artist who moonlights as a mom, author, professor, and sometimes illustrator/graphic designer. Her work is often focused on interpreting aspects of her own personal history as a Hapa/biracial woman. She has an upcoming journal focusing on color theory and her color-meditation practice due out in 2019 with Roost Books.

www.lisasolomon.com

CHRISTINE BUCKTON TILLMAN is primarily a very flat sculptor who draws more often than she makes sculptures. Her main interests as an artist lie in ideas surrounding the handmade, celebrations, and man-made interpretations of natural forms. She earned her BA at Coe College in Cedar Rapids, and earned her MFA from the University of Iowa.

www.christinebucktontillman.com

ABOUT THE AUTHOR

Mixed-media artist and art teacher Susan Schwake is best known for her playful, process-oriented teaching style and for her bold use of color in her nature-inspired paintings. In her own work, she is most interested in the role color plays in nature and often alters or amplifies color to uplift the work or draw attention to overlooked details. Susan has also created several large-scale, site-specific public artworks and permanent exhibits of children's and multi-generational artworks for local municipalities.

She continues to teach art in her little private school called Artstream Studios in New Hampshire and online at www.susanschwake.com.

Susan has written five books about making art with others. Her Art Lab for Kids series is a bestseller—the series has sold over 100,000 copies worldwide and is available in nine languages.

www.susanschwake.com
Instagram: susanbschwake
Facebook: Susan Schwake Art

ACKNOWLEDGMENTS

Big thanks to all the kids who participated in this book and big love to their adults for making it happen. Thanks to the artists in this book's gallery section for sharing their thoughts and work with us! Thanks to Mary Ann Hall for her insight and kindness. Thanks to Renae and David at Quarry for their keen eyes. Endless thanks to my family for their loving support in everything I undertake. Special thanks to all our students and their families at Artstream Studios for helping us build a creative community in our space for all.

THANK YOU TO THE ART LAB KIDS!

Abby, Anna, Audrey, Camarus, Caroline, Charlotte, Cidara, Davis, Drew, Elizabeth, Ethan, Gage, Greta, Gus, Ida, Kaitlyn, Katie, Lila, Lily, Lucy, Lukas, Lydia, Naomi, and Nate.